AUTHENTIC LIVING:

ALIGNING EMOTIONS WITH YOUR TRUE SELF

By Anton Cunningham

Published by Kaja Publishing

ISBN: 979-8-9917451-3-0

Copyright © 2025 by Anton Cunningham and Kaja Publishing, LLC. All rights reserved. No part of this publication may be reproduced, distributed, or transmitted in any form or by any means, including photocopying, recording, or other electronic or mechanical methods, without the prior written permission of the publisher, except in the case of brief quotations embodied in critical reviews and certain other noncommercial uses permitted by copyright law. For permission requests, email to the publisher at anton@kajapublishing.com.

Table of Contents

Introduction

Chapter 1:   2
Understanding Authenticity

Chapter 2:   19
The Concept of Authentic Self vs. Adaptive/Conditioned Self

Chapter 3:   46
The Alignment Process

Chapter 4:   82
Practices for Emotional Authenticity

Chapter 5:   126
Taking One Day at a Time: Integrating Authentic Living into Your Daily Life

INTRODUCTION

You already know what it feels like. That moment when you're saying all the right things while a voice inside whispers: This isn't really me. The exhaustion that comes from maintaining the perfect image. The quiet disappointment of achieving everything you were "supposed to" only to feel strangely empty inside. You're not broken. You're not alone. And that persistent sense that something essential is missing? It's trying to tell you something important.

In a culture fixated on output, genuine authenticity ignites a revolution. This isn't another program for self-optimization; it's a path to liberation, urging you to shed the inauthenticity and rediscover your true self.

This journey isn't about becoming someone new. It's about returning to who you've always been beneath the layers of "shoulds" and expectations. It's about aligning your outer expression with your inner reality, not in some distant future when everything's perfect, but right now, in the beautiful mess of your actual life.

The path isn't always straightforward. You'll encounter resistance, both internal and external. You'll have moments of profound clarity followed by days of forgetting everything you've learned. This is normal. It's human. And with the right tools and perspective, it becomes part of the journey rather than evidence you're doing it wrong.

Your authentic self isn't something you need to create or discover. It's already there, waiting patiently beneath the noise of conditioning and expectation. This book is your invitation to listen to its whisper, to follow its guidance, and to experience the profound relief that comes from finally putting down the weight of who you thought you needed to be.

Are you ready to come home to yourself? Let's begin.

> **"The only way to discover the limits of the possible is to go beyond them into the impossible." - Arthur C. Clarke.**

Chapter 1: Understanding Authenticity

Defining Authenticity

Authenticity is often described as being true to oneself, yet its definition extends beyond mere self-expression. At its core, authenticity involves aligning one's actions, thoughts, and emotions with their core values and beliefs. This alignment encourages a sense of integrity and wholeness, allowing individuals to navigate life with clarity and purpose. Embracing authenticity means cultivating a deeper understanding of our true selves, which can lead to greater emotional intelligence and resilience. By recognizing the importance of authenticity, we can create a more fulfilling and aligned existence.

Authenticity is about living in alignment with your true self, values, and beliefs, rather than conforming to external expectations or pressures. It involves understanding and expressing your genuine thoughts, feelings, and desires, and acting in ways that are consistent with your personal identity and integrity.

Here's a breakdown:

1. **Self-Awareness:** Authenticity starts with a deep understanding of oneself. This includes recognizing your strengths, weaknesses, values, and emotional patterns.
2. **Honest Expression:** Being authentic means expressing your true thoughts, feelings, and preferences in a straightforward and honest manner. This requires courage to be vulnerable and communicate openly.
3. **Consistency:** Living authentically means that your actions consistently reflect your beliefs and values, regardless of the situation or the presence of others.
4. **Autonomy:** Authentic individuals are self-directed and make decisions based on their own values and internal compass, rather than being overly influenced by societal norms or the approval of others.
5. **Integrity:** Authenticity is closely tied to integrity, as it involves being truthful and reliable in your interactions and commitments.

The Science Behind Emotions and Their Purpose

Your Brain on Emotions

Have you ever wondered why a harsh comment from a colleague can ruin your entire day, or why certain songs can instantly transport you back to a specific memory? The answer lies in the remarkable architecture of your brain. Your emotional experiences aren't random reactions—they're sophisticated neurological events orchestrated by specific brain regions working in harmony.

At the center of your emotional responses is your amygdala, a small almond-shaped structure that acts as your brain's emotional alarm system. When you feel that sudden jolt of fear before a public speech or that warm rush of joy when seeing a loved one, your amygdala is actively firing. It's constantly scanning your environment for emotional significance, sometimes before you're even consciously aware of what you're seeing or hearing.

But your emotional experience doesn't end there. Your prefrontal cortex—the area behind your forehead—works like an emotional moderator, helping you make sense of what you're feeling and deciding how to respond. When this relationship between your amygdala and prefrontal cortex is balanced, you experience emotional harmony. When it's not, you might find yourself:

- Overreacting to minor frustrations.
- Dwelling on negative emotions long after the triggering event.
- Making decisions you later regret.
- Feeling emotionally exhausted without understanding why.

Think about a time when you snapped at someone you care about over something insignificant. That moment likely occurred when your amygdala was in overdrive while your prefrontal cortex couldn't keep up. Understanding this neurological dance is your first step toward emotional mastery.

Why We Feel: The Evolutionary Purpose of Emotions

Your emotions aren't design flaws—they're sophisticated survival tools shaped by millions of years of evolution. When you feel afraid, your body prepares to flee danger. When you feel angry, you're mobilizing to protect what's valuable to you. When you feel joy, your brain is reinforcing behaviors that promote your wellbeing.

Imagine walking through your everyday life without these emotional signals. How would you know what's important? How would you connect meaningfully with others? How would you make decisions aligned with what truly matters to you?

Your emotional system serves three critical functions:

1. Survival Messaging: Your emotions provide immediate feedback about your environment, triggering split-second responses that once meant the difference between life and death for your ancestors. Today, this system still works to keep you safe, though the "predators" may now be looming deadlines or relationship conflicts rather than physical dangers.

2. Social Connection: Your capacity for emotions like empathy, compassion, and love enables you to form the deep relationships essential to human flourishing. When you struggle to access or express these emotions, you often experience a profound sense of isolation—even when surrounded by others.

3. Decision Guidance: Every decision you make is influenced by your emotions, whether you realize it or not. Your feelings serve as internal compasses, helping you navigate toward experiences that fulfill your deepest needs and away from those that don't serve your wellbeing.

The pain you feel when disconnected from your emotions isn't just psychological discomfort—it's your system alerting you that something essential is missing. Many people describe this disconnection as feeling "numb," "empty," or like they're "just going through the motions" of life without truly living it.

Emotional Intelligence: Your Path to Authentic Living

Emotional intelligence isn't just another self-improvement trend—it's the science-backed framework that can transform your relationship with yourself and others. Research consistently shows that people with higher emotional intelligence experience:

- Greater career success and higher income
- More satisfying relationships
- Better physical health outcomes
- Higher overall life satisfaction
- Increased resilience during challenging times

The gap between knowing you have emotions and skillfully working with them is where emotional intelligence operates. It's what allows you to transform painful emotional patterns into sources of wisdom and connection.

When Daniel Goleman introduced emotional intelligence to the mainstream in the 1990s, he challenged the prevailing belief that IQ was the primary determinant of success. His research revealed something many of us intuitively sense: your ability to understand and manage emotions—both yours and others'—plays a far greater role in creating a fulfilling life than pure intellectual ability.

Think about the most inspiring person you know. Chances are they embody emotional intelligence—they listen deeply, respond thoughtfully rather than reactively, and seem genuinely connected to themselves and others. This authentic presence isn't accidental; it's cultivated through developing the emotional skills you'll explore in this guide.

The journey to emotional intelligence begins with awareness. As you develop the ability to recognize and name your emotional experiences, you'll discover patterns you may have overlooked for years. This awareness alone can be transformative, creating space between impulse and action where wisdom can emerge.

Your emotions are constantly offering valuable data about what matters to you, what's working in your life, and what needs attention. Learning to access this information without being overwhelmed by it is the first step toward authentic living—and it's a step we'll take together in the pages ahead.

Common Emotional Patterns and Their Impact

The Universal Language of Emotion

Emotions are perhaps the most universal human experience we share. Whether you're in Tokyo, Toronto, or Timbuktu, the fundamental emotions of joy, fear, anger, sadness, disgust, and surprise manifest in remarkably similar ways. They create a common language that transcends cultural boundaries, connecting us in our shared humanity.

What you may not realize, however, is that emotions typically follow patterns—predictable sequences and combinations that shape your internal and external responses. Understanding these patterns is like learning the grammar of your emotional language.

Primary emotions are your immediate, instinctive responses—the initial wave of feeling that arises in response to a situation. Think about the flash of anger when someone cuts you off in traffic or the burst of joy when you receive unexpected good news. These emotions are rapid, automatic, and usually brief in their pure form.

Secondary emotions are what follow—your emotional reactions to your initial emotions. Perhaps you feel guilty about being angry, or anxious about feeling joy because you're waiting for the other shoe to drop. These emotional layers are often where complexity and confusion enter your emotional experience.

> **"I always thought I had an anger problem, but I've realized that anger is often my secondary emotion. What I really feel first is hurt or fear, but those make me feel vulnerable, so I quickly convert them to anger, which feels more empowering in the moment." —Staci Nichole, Previous training client.**

When you become aware of this layering in your emotional experience, you gain tremendous insight into your patterns. You might discover that what you've labeled as "just who I am" is actually a learned emotional sequence that can be understood—and if needed, recalibrated.

When Emotional Patterns Go Wrong

If emotions naturally flow and change, why do so many of us get stuck in painful emotional states? The answer lies in the defensive patterns we develop—often in childhood—that once helped us cope with overwhelming experiences but now limit our emotional freedom.

Let's explore four common dysfunctional patterns that may be operating in your emotional life:

Emotional Suppression: The Bottling Effect

Do you pride yourself on "staying cool" or "not letting things get to you"? While emotional regulation is healthy, suppression—actively pushing emotions down and out of awareness—creates a pressure cooker effect in your mind and body.

Each time you tell yourself "I shouldn't feel this way" or "I need to get over this," you're adding to an invisible emotional debt that eventually demands repayment—often with interest. This might manifest as:

- Unexplained physical symptoms like headaches, digestive issues, or chronic tension.
- Emotional numbness that extends to positive emotions as well as negative ones.
- Unexpected emotional outbursts that seem disproportionate to the triggering event.
- Difficulty connecting deeply with others due to emotional walls.

Suppression is particularly costly because it requires constant energy to maintain. Many people who habitually suppress emotions report feeling exhausted without understanding why.

Rumination: The Mental Hamster Wheel

Have you ever found yourself replaying a conversation or situation over and over, analyzing what went wrong or what you should have said? This pattern—rumination—is one of the most common and least helpful emotional habits.

Rumination tricks you into believing you're solving a problem when you're actually reinforcing neural pathways of distress. It's like wearing a groove in your mental record, making it easier for your thoughts to fall back into the same pattern with each revolution.

The cost of contemplation is steep:

- It prolongs and intensifies negative emotions.
- It increases your risk of anxiety and depression.
- It impairs your ability to think creatively and solve problems.
- It steals your attention from the present moment.

What's particularly insidious about rumination is how reasonable it seems. Your mind presents it as necessary problem-solving rather than the emotional quicksand it actually is.

Emotional Avoidance: The Detour That Becomes the Road

Perhaps the most common pattern I see in my coaching practice is emotional avoidance—structuring your life to minimize contact with uncomfortable emotions. This might look like:

- Keeping extremely busy to avoid quiet moments of reflection.
- Using food, shopping, social media, or substances to change how you feel.
- Automatically changing the subject when conversations get emotionally deep.
- Focusing exclusively on others' needs to avoid examining your own.

The painful irony of avoidance is that it actually expands the territory of what you need to avoid. What begins as sidestepping a specific feeling often grows into avoiding entire categories of experience that might trigger that feeling.

Emotional Reactivity: When Emotions Drive the Car

We all know what it's like to react emotionally in ways we later regret. Emotional reactivity occurs when there's no space between trigger and response—when you go from zero to sixty emotionally without passing through the intervening speeds.

Signs you might be caught in patterns of emotional reactivity include:

- Frequent regret about how you responded in emotional situations.
- Relationships damaged by emotional outbursts.
- A sense that your emotions are unpredictable or beyond your control.
- Others describe you as "too sensitive" or "overreacting".

Reactivity often stems from unexamined triggers—emotional hot buttons installed by past experiences that your current circumstances press without your awareness.

> **"Do not learn how to react. Learn how to respond." - Buddha**

The Real-World Impact of Emotional Patterns

These patterns aren't just psychological curiosities—they shape every dimension of your life in tangible ways. Let me share what research and clinical experience reveal about the far-reaching consequences of unaddressed emotional patterns:

PHYSICAL HEALTH: YOUR BODY KEEPS THE SCORE

Your body doesn't distinguish between emotional and physical threats—both activate your stress response system. Chronic emotional distress creates chronic physiological stress, which is linked to:

- Weakened immune function
- Cardiovascular issues
- Sleep disturbances
- Accelerated cellular aging

If you've ever fallen ill after a period of emotional strain, you've experienced this connection firsthand. Your body literally cannot maintain optimal health while processing ongoing emotional distress.

> **"You must listen to your body. Run, jump, cry, and breathe. Feel the need to express yourself and then find a way to do so that aligns with your character." - Dr. Christine Northrup**

RELATIONSHIP QUALITY: CONNECTIONS THAT NEVER GO DEEP

Authentic relationships require emotional authenticity. When your emotional patterns keep you disconnected from yourself, they inevitably create distance in your relationships as well. This might manifest as:

- Surface-level connections that leave you feeling lonely even when surrounded by people.
- Recurring conflicts that never seem to resolve.
- Difficulty being vulnerable or truly intimate.
- Attracting relationships that reinforce your emotional patterns.

The relationships in your life provide a mirror reflecting your relationship with your own emotions. Creating deeper connections with others begins with creating a deeper connection with yourself.

COGNITIVE PERFORMANCE: THE EMOTIONAL TAX ON YOUR MIND

Your brain's processing power is finite, and unresolved emotional patterns consume cognitive resources that could otherwise be directed toward creative thinking, problem-solving, and focused attention. This "emotional taxation" shows up as:

- Difficulty concentrating
- Impaired decision-making
- Reduced creativity
- Mental fatigue

Have you noticed how hard it is to think clearly when you're emotionally activated? This isn't weakness—it's your brain allocating resources to what it perceives as a more immediate need.

> **"Our bodies are our gardens, to the which our wills are gardeners." - William Shakespeare**

LIFE SATISFACTION: THE GAP BETWEEN LIVING AND THRIVING

Perhaps the most significant impact of unaddressed emotional patterns is on your overall sense of fulfillment. Many people describe it as living at a distance from their own lives—observing rather than fully participating in their experiences.

The good news in all of this? These patterns, though powerful, are not permanent. Each can be transformed through the emotional awareness practices we'll explore throughout this guide. As you develop your capacity to recognize, understand, and work skillfully with your emotions, you'll find yourself naturally shifting toward more authentic ways of being.

In the next section, we'll explore the five core components of emotional intelligence that will serve as your framework for this transformation.

THE FIVE COMPONENTS OF EMOTIONAL INTELLIGENCE

YOUR ROADMAP TO EMOTIONAL MASTERY

Now that you understand the neurological basis of emotions and recognize common emotional patterns, let's explore the practical framework that will guide your journey toward authentic living. Emotional intelligence isn't a single skill but rather a constellation of five interconnected abilities that work together to transform your relationship with emotions.

Think of these five components as different facets of the same gemstone—each reflects light differently, but together they create something of remarkable value. As you develop these capacities, you'll find yourself naturally moving toward more authentic ways of being.

SELF-AWARENESS: THE FOUNDATION OF EVERYTHING

At the core of emotional intelligence lies self-awareness—your ability to recognize and name your emotions as they arise. This sounds deceptively simple, but many of us move through life with only the vaguest sense of our emotional states.

Consider this: Can you distinguish between anxiety and excitement in your body? Between disappointment and sadness? Between irritation and fear? Each has a distinct physical signature and behavioral impact, yet many people lump these experiences into broad categories like "good," "bad," or "stressed."

Self-awareness means developing a nuanced emotional vocabulary and the ability to detect subtle shifts in your internal landscape. It's like upgrading from a basic set of primary colors to a rich palette of shades and hues—suddenly, you can create a more accurate picture of your experience.

When you lack self-awareness, you're essentially navigating your life blindfolded, reacting to emotional triggers without understanding why. This leads to recurring patterns that can feel frustratingly beyond your control.

Ask yourself: On a scale of 1-10, how clearly can you identify what you're feeling in emotionally charged moments? Can you name the specific emotion and locate where you feel it in your body?

> **"What lies behind us and what lies before us are tiny matters compared to what lies within us." - Ralph Waldo Emerson**

SELF-REGULATION: THE ART OF EMOTIONAL NAVIGATION

Self-regulation builds upon self-awareness, adding the crucial capacity to guide your emotional responses rather than being controlled by them. This isn't about suppressing emotions—quite the opposite. Effective self-regulation requires fully acknowledging your feelings while choosing how to express and act upon them.

Think of emotions as powerful currents in the ocean of your experience. Self-regulation is your ability to surf these currents rather than being swept away by them. This might look like:

- Pausing before responding when emotionally triggered.
- Finding healthy ways to process difficult emotions.
- Adapting to changing circumstances with emotional flexibility.
- Staying grounded during uncertainty or stress.

The ability to self-regulate creates freedom in your life. Without it, you're at the mercy of emotional weather patterns, never knowing when a storm might blow you off course. With it, you maintain your direction even through turbulent waters.

Ask yourself: How often do you successfully pause between feeling an emotion and acting on it? Do your emotional responses typically align with your deeper values and goals?

> "Like balancing scales, self-regulation is about adding or removing weights from each side to achieve a stable equilibrium in emotions and actions." - Tavon, Certified Personal Trainer & Coach

MOTIVATION: EMOTIONS AS FUEL FOR GROWTH

Emotional intelligence includes harnessing the motivational power of emotions to move toward meaningful goals. While many people think of motivation as something you either have or don't have, those with high emotional intelligence understand it as an internal resource they can cultivate.

Emotions contain tremendous energy. Fear energizes you to move away from threats, while inspiration energizes you to move toward opportunities. Learning to channel this emotional energy—rather than leaking it through unproductive expressions—is a cornerstone of authentic living.

PEOPLE WITH STRONG EMOTIONAL MOTIVATION:

- Connect their actions to deeper values and purpose
- Maintain enthusiasm through obstacles and setbacks
- Find meaning in challenges rather than just trying to avoid discomfort
- Experience a sense of flow and engagement in their activities

The difference between being moved by external pressures versus internal purpose is profound. The former feels depleting, while the latter generates its own renewable energy.

Ask yourself: Do your goals genuinely inspire you, or are you primarily motivated by avoiding negative outcomes? How connected do you feel to a sense of purpose in your daily activities?

> "Your emotion is nothing but an almighty energy for your motion in pursuit of happiness and achievement." - Toba Beta.

EMPATHY: THE BRIDGE BETWEEN SELF AND OTHERS

Empathy extends your emotional intelligence outward, developing your capacity to recognize and appropriately respond to emotions in others. It's both a cognitive skill (understanding another's perspective) and an emotional skill (feeling with another person).

Without empathy, relationships remain transactional and surface-level. With it, you create spaces of genuine connection where authenticity can flourish. Empathy allows you to:

- Listen beyond words to emotional content

- Validate others' experiences without judgment
- Respond to emotional needs with appropriate support
- Navigate relationship conflicts with compassion

Many people mistakenly believe empathy means agreeing with others or taking responsibility for their emotions. True empathy is simpler and more powerful—it's the ability to temporarily step into another's emotional world while maintaining your own center.

Ask yourself: How often do you find yourself genuinely curious about others' emotional experiences? Can you maintain empathic connection even with those whose perspectives differ from yours?

> **"We think we listen, but very rarely do we listen with real understanding, true empathy. Yet listening, of this very special kind, is one of the most potent forces for change that I know." - Carl Rogers.**

Relationship Management: Authenticity in Action

The final component of emotional intelligence brings together all the others into skillful social interaction. This includes your ability to express yourself authentically, navigate relationships effectively, and create environments where emotional health can thrive.

Social emotional skills manifest as:

- Clear and honest communication about feelings and needs
- Setting healthy boundaries that honor both yourself and others
- Managing conflict as an opportunity for deeper understanding
- Building and maintaining meaningful connections

These skills aren't about social manipulation or impression management—quite the opposite. They enable you to show up as your true self while creating space for others to do the same.

Ask yourself: Do your relationships reflect your authentic self? Can you express your needs and boundaries clearly while remaining connected to others?

The Integrated Experience of Emotional Intelligence

While we've explored these five components separately for clarity, in practice they work together as an integrated whole. Self-awareness enables self-regulation, which supports motivation, which deepens empathy, which enhances social skills—and the cycle continues in an upward spiral of emotional development.

Imagine emotional intelligence as a complex, interconnected system. It's not about mastering one aspect and neglecting another. It's a holistic integration, where self-awareness seamlessly blends with empathy, and where skillful relationship management arises from a deep understanding of both internal and external landscapes. It's the fluid interplay of self-regulation, motivation, and social awareness that defines its power. Each element enhances and is enhanced by the others, resulting in a dynamic and adaptive form of intelligence. This integrated experience allows for better responses, fostering genuine connection and effective action in any context.

As you progress through this guide, you'll have opportunities to strengthen each of these components. You'll likely discover that you're naturally stronger in some areas than others—most people are. The beauty of this framework is that by strengthening your weaker areas, you automatically enhance the functioning of the entire system.

In the next section, we'll explore how to recognize the specific triggers that activate your emotional patterns, creating the awareness that makes transformation possible.

Recognizing Emotional Triggers and Reactions

The Moments That Matter Most

You're having a perfectly pleasant day when suddenly—a comment from your partner, an email from your boss, or even a social media post—sends you into an emotional tailspin. Why do certain situations affect you so powerfully while others don't register at all? The answer lies in understanding your unique emotional triggers.

Emotional triggers are specific events, comments, or situations that reliably activate strong emotional responses in you. They're like buttons installed by your past experiences—when pressed, they automatically launch specific emotional programs. Recognizing these triggers is perhaps the most practical and immediately useful aspect of emotional intelligence.

The Anatomy of a Trigger

To work effectively with triggers, you need to understand their components. Every emotional trigger scenario typically includes:

1. The activating event (what actually happened).
2. Your perception and interpretation (the meaning you assign).
3. Your emotional response (what you feel).
4. Your behavioral reaction (what you do).

The pain of being triggered comes not just from the unpleasant emotions but from the sense of being controlled by your reactions—of following the same script despite your best intentions to respond differently.

Let's look at a common example:

> Activating event: Your partner is late coming home and doesn't call
>
> Your interpretation: "They don't respect my time or care about my feelings"
>
> Emotional response: Anger, hurt, anxiety
>
> Behavioral reaction: Cold shoulder, sarcastic comments, interrogation about where they've been

The power of this cycle lies in its automaticity—it can unfold in seconds, bypassing your conscious awareness entirely. But with practice, you can learn to insert brief moments of awareness that interrupt the automatic sequence, creating space for choice.

Mapping Your Trigger Territory

Your emotional triggers aren't random—they fall into recognizable categories that reflect your core needs, values, and past experiences. The four most common trigger categories include:

1. Past Wounds and Trauma

When current situations echo past painful experiences, they can trigger disproportionate emotional responses. These triggers often activate your survival brain, creating reactions that seem essential in the moment but are actually responding to the past rather than the present.

Signs you're experiencing a trauma-based trigger:

- The intensity of emotion seems much stronger than the situation warrants.

- You feel younger or more vulnerable than usual.
- You experience physical fight-flight-freeze symptoms (racing heart, tight chest, inability to think clearly).
- You have the sense of being "back there" rather than fully in the present.

2. Unmet Core Needs

Every human has fundamental needs for safety, connection, autonomy, and meaning. When these needs are threatened or appear to be at risk, strong emotions naturally arise as a protective response.

Common need-based triggers include:

- Feeling excluded or left out (threatening belonging needs)
- Having your competence questioned (threatening esteem needs)
- Being controlled or micromanaged (threatening autonomy needs)
- Facing unpredictable circumstances (threatening safety/security needs)

The emotions triggered by unmet needs aren't problems to be fixed—they're valuable signals highlighting what matters most to you.

3. Value Violations

Your values—what you believe is important and right—form an invisible framework through which you interpret the world. When you witness or experience something that contradicts these core values, emotional triggers are commonly activated.

For example:

- If you deeply value honesty, even small deceptions may trigger strong reactions
- If you value fairness, witnessing favoritism might ignite your anger
- If you value achievement, feeling held back can trigger frustration or despair

These value-based triggers often reveal what you care about most deeply, even if you haven't consciously articulated these values to yourself.

4. Present Stressors and Vulnerabilities

Sometimes triggers aren't about the past or deep-seated values but simply reflect your current capacity and circumstances. When you're already stressed, sleep-deprived, hungry, or overwhelmed, your threshold for emotional activation naturally lowers.

This explains why you might handle criticism gracefully on one day and be devastated by a milder comment the next. Your emotional responses always exist in the context of your current resources and resilience.

> **"Understanding your triggers isn't about placing blame, but taking responsibility for your emotional reactions."**

THE GAP: WHERE FREEDOM LIVES

Between every trigger and reaction lies a space—what psychologist Viktor Frankl called "the last of human freedoms"—the ability to choose your response rather than react automatically. This gap might be milliseconds at first, but with practice, it can expand into a meaningful pause where awareness and choice become possible.

Cultivating this gap involves:

- **Noticing physical cues:** Your body always responds to triggers before your conscious mind registers them. Learning to recognize your unique physiological signatures of activation (tension in specific areas, changes in breathing, shifts in posture) gives you early warning signals.
- **Naming what's happening:** The simple act of mentally noting "I'm being triggered right now" can interrupt the automatic cycle, activating your prefrontal cortex and dampening the amygdala's alarm.
- **Remembering you have options:** In triggered moments, your perspective narrows dramatically, making it seem like there's only one possible response. Reminding yourself "I have choices here" reopens your awareness to alternatives.
- **Using pattern interrupts:** Simple actions like taking a deep breath, feeling your feet on the ground, or silently counting to ten can break the momentum of an emerging reaction.

The path to emotional freedom doesn't require you to prevent triggers—that's neither possible nor desirable. Instead, it involves developing your capacity to navigate triggered moments with increasing awareness and flexibility.

> **"Between stimulus and response there is a space. In that space is our power to choose our response. In our response lies our growth and our freedom." - Viktor E. Frankl.**

BEGINNING YOUR TRIGGER TRACKING PRACTICE

The first step in working skillfully with triggers is simply becoming more aware of them. A consistent practice of noticing and naming your triggers—without judgment or immediate attempts to change them—builds the foundation for everything that follows.

Here's a simple daily practice to begin with:

1. At the end of each day, reflect on moments when you felt emotionally activated
2. For each instance, note:
    - What was happening right before the emotional shift?
    - What thoughts went through your mind?
    - What emotions arose?
    - How did you respond behaviorally?
    - What might the trigger be revealing about your needs or values?

This reflective practice gradually builds your "trigger literacy"—your ability to read and understand the emotional patterns specific to your life. As this awareness grows, you'll likely notice recurring themes and situations, giving you valuable information about where to focus your attention.

As we conclude this chapter on understanding your emotional landscape, remember that awareness itself is transformative. Simply by shining the light of your attention on these patterns, you've already begun the process of change. In the chapters ahead, we'll build on this foundation, exploring how to distinguish between your authentic self and conditioned responses, and developing practical skills for emotional alignment in everyday life.

You've taken the first and perhaps most crucial step on the journey toward emotional alignment—recognizing that the disconnection you've felt isn't a personal failing but a natural consequence of how we learn to navigate a complex world. Your emotions, even the difficult ones, aren't problems to be solved but messengers carrying important information about your needs, values, and authentic experience.

The patterns you've recognized through this chapter—whether emotional suppression, rumination, or reactivity—developed for good reasons. They were your best attempts to protect yourself with the resources available at the time. Acknowledging these patterns with compassion creates the foundation for change that criticism never could.

As we move forward to explore the distinction between your authentic and conditioned selves in the next chapter, carry this newfound awareness with you. Notice the subtle shifts in how you relate to your emotions—the moments of recognition, the brief pauses before reaction, the gentle curiosity about what your feelings might be telling you.

These small changes may seem insignificant, but they signal the beginning of a seismic shift in your relationship with your emotional world. Each moment of awareness creates a small opening between stimulus and response, between old patterns and new possibilities—an opening through which your authentic self can gradually emerge.

Chapter 2: The Concept of Authentic Self vs. Adaptive/Conditioned Self

Have you ever found yourself nodding along in a conversation while thinking something completely different? Or laughing at a joke that didn't actually amuse you? Or perhaps you've achieved everything you were "supposed to" only to feel strangely empty inside?

Welcome to the universal experience of living from your conditioned self.

It happens in those moments when you automatically say "I'm fine" despite feeling anything but fine. When you scroll through your own social media and barely recognize the person being portrayed. When you lie awake at night wondering if anyone knows who you really are—including yourself.

You're not alone. In a world that rewards performance over presence, countless others share your experience:

- The high-achieving professional who's built an impressive career but can't shake the feeling they're living someone else's definition of success.
- The social chameleon who knows exactly how to fit in everywhere but belongs nowhere.
- The perfectionist whose endless self-criticism drowns out any genuine sense of accomplishment.
- The chronic people-pleaser who's so attuned to others' needs they've lost touch with their own.

This gap between who you really are and who you've learned to be isn't a character flaw—it's the natural result of growing up in a world that sent clear messages about what made you acceptable, lovable, and safe. Your conditioned self developed as an intelligent adaptation to your environment, a sophisticated strategy for belonging and survival.

But the protection it once provided now comes at a cost. Living from conditioning creates a persistent sense of disconnection—from yourself, from others, from the direct experience of your life. It's exhausting to maintain and ultimately unsatisfying, no matter how successful it appears from the outside.

The good news? Beneath these layers of conditioning, your authentic self remains intact. This chapter isn't about discovering who you "should" be but recognizing who you already are beneath the strategies and masks you've accumulated. Understanding the difference between your authentic and conditioned selves creates the foundation for everything that follows.

Discovering the Two Selves Within

Have you ever felt like you were playing a role rather than truly being yourself? Perhaps in certain situations—a work meeting, a family gathering, or even a casual social event—you notice yourself saying and doing things that don't quite feel like "you." This common experience points to one of the most significant insights in emotional intelligence: within each of us exist two distinct ways of being that I call the authentic self and the conditioned self.

The concept of the authentic self versus the adaptive/conditioned self explores the tension between our intrinsic nature and the personas we develop to navigate the world. The authentic self represents our core values, desires, and inherent traits, unburdened by external pressures. Conversely, the adaptive/conditioned self is a collection of behaviors and beliefs learned through societal expectations, past traumas, and survival mechanisms. While necessary for social functioning, over-reliance on the conditioned self can lead to dissonance and a sense of disconnection from our true selves. The journey towards authenticity involves discerning which aspects of our identity are genuine and which are learned adaptations, allowing us to live more aligned with our core.

Understanding this internal division is like finding a map when you've been lost in the woods. Suddenly, the confusing terrain of your emotional life begins to make sense. The contradictions, the inexplicable reactions, the moments of feeling disconnected from yourself—all can be understood through this powerful framework.

Your Authentic Self: The Original You

At your core exists an authentic self that has been present since your earliest days. This isn't a mystical concept but a practical reality of human development. Your authentic self embodies your natural tendencies, genuine emotions, and inherent values before external conditioning shaped your responses to the world.

Think back to the natural curiosity and wonder you likely experienced as a young child—the spontaneous laughter, the honest expression of feelings, the natural pursuit of what interested you. These qualities reflect your authentic self in its purest form.

> **"There is nothing more beautiful than seeing a person being themselves. Imagine going through your day being unapologetically you."** - Steve Maraboli.

Your authentic self is characterized by several key qualities:

- **Present-moment awareness** — Being fully engaged with your current experience.
- **Emotional honesty** — Feeling and expressing emotions as they naturally arise.
- **Internal guidance** — Making choices based on what feels right from within.

- **Natural curiosity** — Genuine interest in exploring and understanding.
- **Spontaneity** — Actions that arise naturally rather than from calculation.
- **Self-compassion** — A kind, accepting attitude toward your own experience.

When operating from your authentic self, you'll notice a distinct sense of alignment—what you think, feel, say, and do all come from the same source. This alignment creates a feeling of integrity that's both grounding and energizing.

The authentic self serves as your internal guidance system—a reliable compass pointing toward what's truly important to you. You've likely experienced moments when, despite external pressure or logical arguments to the contrary, something inside you simply knew what was right for you. That knowing comes from your authentic self.

Perhaps the most remarkable quality of your authentic self is its consistency through life's changes. While your interests, relationships, and circumstances naturally evolve, the core qualities of your authentic self remain surprisingly stable. The passions of a five-year-old often contain the seeds of an adult's deepest values and purposes.

Your Conditioned Self: The Adaptive Protector

If your authentic self is your original nature, your conditioned self is what developed to help you adapt through the complex social world. It represents the collection of adaptations, beliefs, and behaviors you learned to keep yourself safe, gain acceptance, and meet your needs in your particular environment.

This conditioning begins the moment you enter the world and accelerates as you grow. Through countless interactions, you learn what brings approval and what triggers rejection:

- The emotions that get positive responses versus those that are discouraged.
- The aspects of yourself that earn praise versus those that provoke criticism.
- The behaviors that are rewarded versus those that are punished.

Your conditioned self forms as a response to these experiences, creating protective patterns that help you manage your specific family system, cultural context, and social environment.

> **"Until you make the unconscious conscious, it will direct your life and you will call it fate." - Carl Jung.**

It's crucial to understand that your conditioned self isn't a villain or an impostor—it's a necessary and intelligent adaptation that helped you survive and thrive. When you were young and dependent on others for your basic needs, gaining acceptance wasn't just about fitting in; it was fundamentally about safety and survival.

Common conditioned patterns include:

- **People-pleasing** — Prioritizing others' needs and approval over your own feelings.
- **Perfectionism** — Setting impossibly high standards to avoid criticism or rejection.
- **Achievement orientation** — Defining your worth through accomplishments.
- **Emotional suppression** — Hiding feelings deemed unacceptable or inconvenient.
- **Hypervigilance** — Constantly scanning for potential threats or disapproval.
- **Role adaptation** — Becoming who others need or expect you to be.

These patterns aren't character flaws or weaknesses—they're sophisticated survival strategies that worked in the past. The pain they cause emerges not from their existence but from their persistence long after they've served their purpose.

Think about it this way. That voice in your head that tells you to always be "on," to never mess up, to keep everyone happy? That wasn't born from weakness. It was actually pretty smart. When you were little and your whole world depended on the adults around you, figuring out how to fit in wasn't just about being liked—it was about making sure your basic needs got met. So you watched closely and adapted. Maybe you learned that being perfect kept the peace, or that hiding certain feelings made people more comfortable, or that achievements were the surest way to get attention. These weren't bad strategies! They probably worked really well back then. The problem isn't that you developed these patterns—it's that they're still running the show now, in situations where they're no longer needed. It's like having an overprotective bodyguard who made total sense in a dangerous neighborhood but is now tackling the mailman on your safe suburban street. Understanding this isn't about beating yourself up—it's about recognizing an old solution that's become a new problem.

> **"Be who you are and say what you feel, because those who mind don't matter, and those who matter don't mind." - Bernard M. Baruch.**

THE DANCE BETWEEN BOTH SELVES

Rather than thinking of your authentic and conditioned selves as separate entities locked in combat, it's more accurate and helpful to view them as different aspects of you engaged in a complex dance. They interact continuously, with one or the other taking the lead depending on the context and your level of awareness.

This interaction often takes the form of an internal dialogue:

- Your authentic self feels drawn toward a new creative pursuit, while your conditioned self warns about potential failure and embarrassment.
- Your authentic self notices hurt in a relationship, while your conditioned self insists you shouldn't make waves.

- Your authentic self feels tired and needs rest, while your conditioned self pushes you to keep working to prove your worth.

The conditioned self speaks the language of "should," "must," and "have to," while the authentic self communicates through feelings, intuitions, and natural inclinations. Learning to distinguish these voices is a important skill in emotional intelligence.

Different situations can trigger either your authentic or conditioned self to take prominence:

- High-stress environments often activate conditioned responses.
- Safe, accepting relationships may allow your authentic self to come out.
- New situations might intensify conditioned patterns due to uncertainty.
- Creative activities often provide channels for authentic expression.

The pain of living primarily from your conditioned self manifests as a deep-rooted disconnection—from your emotions, your body, your desires, and ultimately from the people around you. This disconnection often feels like:

- Going through the motions of life without genuine engagement.
- Making choices that look good on paper but leave you feeling empty.
- Achieving goals that don't bring the satisfaction you expected.
- Maintaining relationships that feel performative rather than true.

This pain isn't merely psychological—it's physiological. Living in contradiction to your authentic nature creates chronic stress that affects every system in your body. Your nervous system recognizes the dissonance between your outer presentation and inner reality, even when your conscious mind has normalized it.

The Journey of Return

The relationship between your authentic and conditioned selves isn't a problem to solve once and for all but rather a lifelong journey of increasing awareness and integration. This journey should not be about eliminating your conditioned self—which would be neither possible nor desirable—but about bringing it into conscious relationship with your authentic core.

This integration process involves:

1. **Recognizing** when you're operating from conditioning rather than authenticity.
2. **Honoring** the protective intention behind conditioned patterns.
3. **Reconnecting** with the authentic feelings and needs beneath the conditioning.
4. **Choosing** responses that honor both your authenticity and your real-world context.

The joy of this integration process is the great relief of coming home to yourself. When your outer expression aligns with your inner reality, the energy previously spent maintaining the gap becomes available for creative expression, meaningful connection, and genuine engagement with life.

People who've reclaimed aspects of their authentic self often describe it as:

- "Finally being able to exhale fully".
- "Dropping a burden I didn't realize I was carrying".
- "Coming back into my body after being absent for years".
- "Feeling like myself for the first time since childhood".

This path toward authenticity doesn't mean you'll never again act from conditioning—you will, because you're human. The difference is that with awareness, these moments become conscious choices rather than automatic reactions. You gain the freedom to draw on conditioned skills when they serve you while staying connected to your authentic core.

> **"To be nobody but yourself in a world which is doing its best, night and day, to make you everybody else means to fight the hardest battle which any human being can fight; and never stop fighting." - E.E. Cummings.**

How Societal Expectations Shape Our Emotional Responses

The Invisible Hands That Mold Your Emotions

While we often think of our emotional responses as purely personal, the truth is far more complex. Your emotional landscape has been shaped by countless external influences—some obvious, others nearly invisible. Understanding these forces doesn't diminish your personal responsibility for your emotions, but it does offer compassionate context for why you feel and respond the way you do.

Imagine growing up in a vastly different culture, family, or era—your emotional responses would likely be dramatically different. This isn't because your authentic self would be different, but because the conditioning surrounding your emotions would have taken a different form.

Cultural Blueprints for Emotional Expression

Every culture creates unwritten rules about which emotions are acceptable, how intensely they should be expressed, and in what contexts. These "emotional display rules" vary tremendously across different societies but are typically absorbed so early in life that they feel like natural laws rather than cultural constructs.

Consider how these cultural patterns might be influencing your emotional life:

- **Emotional Hierarchy** — In Western cultures, happiness and excitement are typically valued above sadness or fear, creating an implicit pressure to "be positive." How might this hierarchy affect your willingness to acknowledge more challenging emotions?
- **Expression Intensity** — Some cultures encourage animated emotional expression, while others prize emotional restraint. Where did your family and community fall on this spectrum, and how has this shaped your comfort with emotional intensity?
- **Contextual Appropriateness** — Every culture has unwritten rules about where and when certain emotions can be expressed. Think about the emotional rules in various contexts in your life—work meetings, family gatherings, religious settings. How do these vary?

The pain of cultural conditioning comes when your natural emotional responses conflict with these unwritten rules. You might find yourself feeling guilty for emotions that are perfectly natural, or suppressing feelings that need expression, simply because they don't align with your cultural blueprint.

The Gendered Landscape of Emotion

Perhaps no aspect of emotional conditioning is more powerful than gender expectations. From early childhood, most people receive consistent messages about which emotions are appropriate for their gender, creating profound influences on emotional development.

Common gendered emotional patterns in many Western cultures include:

Traditional Masculine Conditioning:

- Anger is more acceptable than fear or sadness.
- Emotional restraint is valued over expression.
- Vulnerability is associated with weakness.
- Pride and confidence are encouraged.

Traditional Feminine Conditioning:

- Caregiving emotions like empathy are emphasized.
- Anger is often discouraged or redirected.
- Expression of fear and sadness is more acceptable.
- Emotions that take up space may be labeled "too much".

These patterns aren't universal or absolute, and they're evolving in many communities. However, their influence remains powerful, often operating below the level of conscious awareness. The emotional aspects of yourself that don't fit these gendered expectations may have been pushed into the shadows of your conditioned self.

The cost of this gendered emotional conditioning is enormous. Research consistently shows that emotional suppression—regardless of which specific emotions are being suppressed—is linked to reduced wellbeing, poorer health outcomes, and less satisfying relationships.

> **"Emotions have no gender. What we have is emotional gender stereotypes that we need to fight." - Unknown.**

Your Family's Emotional Inheritance

While culture and gender create broad patterns, your family system provided the immediate environment where your emotional conditioning took shape. Family systems have their own emotional rules, often passed down through generations:

- Which emotions were welcomed, tolerated, or rejected in your family?
- How did the adults around you handle their own emotions?
- What emotional roles did different family members play? (The peacemaker, the explosive one, the stoic one, etc.)
- What went unspoken or was considered emotionally off-limits?

Your family's approach to emotions wasn't just taught through explicit instructions but modeled in thousands of interactions. You learned by watching how emotions were handled—or not handled—by the people around you.

One of the most powerful aspects of family emotional conditioning is what psychologists call "emotional contingencies." These are the unspoken connections between your emotional expressions and whether you received love, attention, and care. Perhaps you learned that:

- Being happy and compliant brought attention and approval
- Strong emotions led to abandonment or rejection
- Caregiving for others' emotions earned you connection
- Certain feelings made adults uncomfortable and were best hidden

These early emotional contingencies create deeply ingrained patterns that can persist long into adulthood, affecting everything from your intimate relationships to your career choices.

The Workplace and Professional Persona

As an adult, your emotional conditioning continues to be shaped by professional environments, each with their own emotional culture:

- Corporate settings often prize analytical thinking over emotional awareness
- Service industries may require "emotional labor"—displaying emotions you don't feel
- Creative fields might value passion but still have specific rules about its expression
- Healthcare environments may emphasize empathy while requiring emotional boundaries

These professional emotional rules can create what sociologists call "emotional dissonance"—the stressful gap between what you actually feel and what you're expected to display. Over time, this dissonance can disconnect you from your authentic emotional responses, as your work persona becomes increasingly automatic.

The Inner Critic as Society's Voice

One of the most powerful ways societal expectations shape your emotions is through the development of your inner critic—that internal voice of judgment and evaluation that comments on your emotional responses.

Your inner critic didn't originate within you. It's an internalized collection of external voices and standards that you've absorbed throughout your life. When your inner critic says things like:

- "You shouldn't feel that way"
- "What's wrong with you?"
- "No one wants to hear about your problems"
- "You're too sensitive/not sensitive enough"

It's actually repeating messages from your social environment that you've taken in and made your own. Understanding this can help you relate to self-criticism with greater compassion, recognizing that these judgments reflect conditioned patterns rather than objective truth.

> **"If you hear a voice within you say 'you cannot paint,' then by all means paint, and that voice will be silenced." - Vincent Van Gogh.**

Media and Technology: The Modern Emotional Influencers

In today's culture, traditional sources of emotional conditioning are joined by powerful new influences through media and technology:

- **Social Media Comparison** — Curated emotional presentations that create unrealistic standards.
- **Attention Economy** — Platforms designed to trigger emotional reactions for engagement.
- **Digital Emotional Performance** — The pressure to display certain emotions publicly.
- **Accelerated Emotional Cycles** — The increasing speed of emotional trends and reactions.

These modern influences can intensify emotional conditioning, as they provide constant feedback about which emotional expressions receive validation in the form of likes, shares, and comments.

Finding Freedom Within Conditioning

Understanding these societal influences on your emotions isn't about assigning blame or rejecting all cultural standards. Rather, it's about developing the awareness that allows you to make conscious choices about which aspects of conditioning serve your authentic self and which do not.

This awareness creates freedom—not freedom from conditioning, which is impossible, but freedom to relate to conditioning with discernment. With this understanding, you can:

- Recognize when you're responding from societal expectations rather than internal truth.
- Compassionately understand your emotional reactions in their full context.
- Challenge emotional "rules" that don't serve your wellbeing.
- Create environments that support more authentic emotional expression.

The journey toward emotional authenticity doesn't mean rejecting all cultural influences—that would simply be replacing one form of conditioning with another. Instead, it means developing a conscious relationship with these influences, allowing your authentic self to engage with them from a place of choice rather than automatic compliance.

As we move into the next section, we'll explore how to recognize when you're living primarily from your conditioned self, identifying specific signs that can alert you to this disconnection from authenticity.

Signs of Living from Your Conditioned Self

Recognizing When You're Disconnected from Authenticity

Now that you understand how your authentic and conditioned selves developed, let's explore how to recognize when you're operating primarily from conditioning rather than authenticity. This awareness is the essential first step toward reclaiming your emotional wholeness.

The signs of living from your conditioned self aren't personality flaws or weaknesses—they're valuable signals pointing toward areas where reconnection with your authentic self is possible. Each signal represents an opportunity for greater alignment and freedom.

> **"Listen to your own voice, your own soul. Too many people listen to the noise of the world, instead of themselves." - Leon Brown.**

Emotional Indicators: What Your Feelings Are Telling You

Your emotions themselves provide the most direct information about your relationship with authenticity. Pay particular attention to these emotional experiences that often indicate conditioning is in the driver's seat:

Persistent Emptiness: The Hollow Center

Perhaps the most common emotional signature of living from your conditioned self is a pervasive sense of emptiness—a feeling that something essential is missing despite having the external elements of a good life. This emptiness can manifest as:

- A nagging sense that "there must be more than this."
- Feeling like you're going through the motions of life.
- A disconnection between achievements and satisfaction.
- Wondering if something is fundamentally wrong with you.

This emptiness isn't a character defect or a sign of ungratefulness—it's your authentic self signaling its absence from your conscious experience. It's a healthy response to an unhealthy situation: living a life that doesn't reflect your deeper truth.

Emotional Numbing: When Feeling Becomes Dangerous

Another clear indicator is a generalized numbing or dampening of your emotional experience. While this numbing often begins as a protective strategy to avoid painful emotions, it eventually limits your access to positive emotions as well.

You might recognize emotional numbing if you:

- Have difficulty identifying what you're feeling
- Experience emotions as distant or muted
- Notice stronger emotional responses to fiction than to your own life
- Feel generally disconnected from your body

The painful irony of emotional numbing is that while it initially develops to protect you from overwhelming feelings, it eventually becomes a source of suffering itself—cutting you off from the key information and energy your emotions provide.

> **"Emotions are temporary states of mind, don't let them permanently destroy you!"**

DISPROPORTIONATE REACTIONS: WHEN PAST MEETS PRESENT

When you're operating from your conditioned self, you're likely to experience emotional reactions that seem disproportionate to current circumstances. These reactions occur because present situations are activating old emotional patterns from your past.

Signs of these disproportionate reactions include:

- Finding yourself suddenly enraged by minor irritations
- Feeling devastated by small disappointments
- Experiencing anxiety in objectively safe situations
- Having the sense of being "hijacked" by your emotions

These reactions often contain important clues about your earliest emotional conditioning. The intensity of your response usually reflects not just the present trigger but the accumulated weight of similar experiences throughout your life.

> **"Your past is important, but it is not nearly as important to your present as the way you see your future." - Tony Robbins.**

EMOTIONAL EXHAUSTION: THE ENERGY DRAIN OF INCONGRUENCE

Living from your conditioned self requires enormous energy—the constant effort of monitoring, adjusting, and performing takes a toll that manifests as chronic emotional fatigue. This isn't the healthy tiredness that follows meaningful exertion but a deeper depletion.

You might be experiencing this kind of exhaustion if you:

- Feel drained after social interactions where you "performed" well.
- Need excessive recovery time from ordinary activities.
- Experience a sense of relief when plans are canceled.
- Find yourself too depleted to engage with activities you apparently enjoy.

This exhaustion signals the unsustainable energy cost of maintaining a space between your inner reality and outer presentation. Your system is telling you it cannot indefinitely support this level of incongruence.

> **"Almost everything will work again if you unplug it for a few minutes, including you." - Anne Lamott.**

Cognitive Signs: How Your Thinking Patterns Reveal Conditioning

Beyond emotions, your thought patterns offer clear indicators of when you're operating from conditioning rather than authenticity.

Rigid Thinking: The Tyranny of Should

One of the most reliable signs of conditioned thinking is the prevalence of rigid, rule-bound thoughts dominated by words like "should," "must," "always," and "never." These thoughts reflect internalized external standards rather than your authentic values.

Examples of this rigid thinking include:

- "I should be further along in my career by now."
- "I must never let others see my vulnerability."
- "People always take advantage of kindness."
- "I never deserve to rest until everything is perfect."

The pain of these thought patterns comes from their inflexibility and disconnection from context. They apply universal rules to unique situations, creating impossible standards that set you up for endless inadequacy.

EXTERNAL REFERENCING: LOOKING OUTSIDE FOR INNER ANSWERS

Another cognitive sign of living from your conditioned self is excessive external referencing—consistently looking outside yourself to determine how you should feel, what you should want, and what choices you should make.

This pattern might show up as:

- Inability to make decisions without extensive consultation.
- Changing your opinion to match those around you.
- Reflexively checking social media for how to respond to events.
- Prioritizing expert advice over your own experience.

Yes, seeking input from others can be valuable, external referencing becomes problematic when it consistently overrides your internal wisdom. Your authentic self gets lost in the noise of others' opinions.

DECISION PARALYSIS: WHEN CHOICES BECOME OVERWHELMING

When disconnected from your authentic self, decision-making often becomes extraordinarily difficult. Without clear access to your genuine preferences and values, even simple choices can feel overwhelming.

Signs of decision paralysis include:

- Agonizing over minor decisions.
- Feeling equally pulled in multiple directions.
- Making choices based on what will cause least regret rather than what you want.
- Frequently changing your mind after decisions are made.

This paralysis stems from the absence of your authentic self as an internal guide. Without that compass, every option seems equally valid (or invalid), making confident choice nearly impossible.

> **"It's not the overload of information that's the problem, it's the overload of choices that paralyzes us." - Barry Schwartz.**

MENTAL LOOPS: THE HAMSTER WHEEL OF RUMINATION

Living from your conditioned self often involves persistent thought patterns that circle without resolution. These mental loops typically center on concerns about performance, acceptance, or control.

Common rumination themes include:

- Replaying past interactions, looking for mistakes.
- Rehearsing future scenarios to prevent possible failure.
- Comparing yourself to others and finding yourself lacking.
- Questioning whether your feelings are valid or acceptable.

These mental loops consume tremendous cognitive energy while rarely producing useful insights. They're the mind's attempt to control what can only be resolved through reconnection with your authentic experience.

> **"You can't think yourself out of a problem you behaved yourself into." - Stephen Covey.**

Behavioral Patterns: What Your Actions Reveal

Your behavior provides some of the most observable evidence of whether you're living from your authentic or conditioned self.

Inconsistent Actions: The Chameleon Effect

One clear behavioral sign is dramatic variation in how you act depending on who you're with. While some contextual adaptation is natural and appropriate, significant inconsistency suggests your behavior is being driven by others' expectations rather than your internal guide.

This inconsistency might look like:

- Having a "work personality" dramatically different from your "home personality."
- Changing your opinions based on who you're talking to.
- Adjusting your appearance for different social groups.
- Finding that friends from different parts of your life would barely recognize you with others.

This chameleon-like adaptation is initially a sophisticated social skill, but when taken to extremes, it disconnects you from a consistent sense of self.

COMPULSIVE PATTERNS: WHEN BEHAVIORS CONTROL YOU

Another behavioral indicator is engagement in compulsive activities that feel automatic rather than chosen. These behaviors often serve to manage uncomfortable emotions or create a sense of control.

Common compulsive patterns include:

- Workaholism or busyness that prevents quiet reflection.
- Excessive social media checking or digital distraction.
- Rigid routines that feel mandatory rather than supportive.
- Compulsive spending, eating, or other consumption habits.

The sure sign of these behaviors isn't the activities themselves but your relationship to them—they feel necessary rather than freely chosen, and attempts to change them trigger significant anxiety.

AVOIDANCE STRATEGIES: THE PATHS NOT TAKEN

Living from your conditioned self typically involves elaborate strategies to avoid particular experiences, emotions, or situations. These avoidance patterns limit your life options and keep you in familiar but restricted territory.

Signs of avoidance-based living include:

- Consistently steering conversations away from certain topics.
- Procrastinating on activities that might trigger uncomfortable feelings.
- Using substances or activities to change or numb emotional states.
- Creating elaborate justifications for not pursuing meaningful goals.

These avoidance strategies provide short-term emotional relief but long-term limitation, gradually narrowing your life to exclude anything that might trigger conditioned fears.

> **"Life is a sum of all your choices." - Albert Camus.**

ACHIEVEMENT WITHOUT FULFILLMENT: THE EMPTY SUCCESS

Perhaps one of the most pitiful behavioral signs is the pursuit and attainment of goals that bring little genuine satisfaction. This pattern reveals a disconnect between your conditioned definition of success and what truly matters to your authentic self.

This might manifest as:

- Achieving important milestones and feeling nothing.

- Constantly moving the goalposts of what counts as "enough."
- Success that impresses others but leaves you cold.
- The sense that you're living someone else's definition of a good life.

This pattern is particularly challenging because external validation often reinforces behaviors that don't actually serve your deeper satisfaction.

"There is no real success without fulfillment." - Deepak Chopra.

Relational Manifestations: How Connections Reflect Conditioning

Finally, your relationships offer a mirror reflecting your relationship with yourself, showing clear signs of when you're operating from conditioning rather than authenticity.

Relational manifestations reveal how our conditioning shapes our connections. The patterns we establish in relationships often mirror the learned behaviors and emotional responses developed in our formative years. If we were conditioned to seek approval, we might become people-pleasers; if we experienced abandonment, we might struggle with trust. These manifestations aren't just about individual quirks; they're the tangible expressions of our internal landscapes, playing out in the dynamics of our friendships, partnerships, and family ties. By observing these relational patterns, we gain valuable insights into our conditioning and create opportunities for conscious change.

Role-Playing in Relationships: The Assigned Parts

Okay, so, think about it like this: ever feel like you're playing a character in your own life, especially with people you're close to? Like, you're always the "strong one" or the "funny one," even when you're not feeling it? That's kind of what it is to live from that conditioned self. You're stuck in these roles, like someone handed you a script, and you just keep reading the same lines. You might notice it's hard to be vulnerable, or that people only seem to see you for what you do for them, not just you being you. And man, doesn't it feel good when you finally get to be alone and just... relax, without having to "perform"? That's because those roles, while they might have helped you survive back in the day, are now keeping you from having real, honest connections.

When living from your conditioned self, your relationships often feel like role performances rather than authentic connections. You find yourself slipping into familiar parts—the helper, the rock, the achiever, the peacemaker—rather than showing up as your full self.

Signs of role-playing include:

- Feeling like you can only show certain aspects of yourself.
- Relationships that follow predictable scripts.
- Being valued for what you provide rather than who you are.
- Relief when you can "drop the act" after social interactions.

These roles initially developed to help you meet emotional needs in your early environment, but they now limit the depth and authenticity of your connections.

Difficulty with Boundaries: Too Rigid or Too Open

Boundary challenges strongly indicate conditioning is at work, whether those boundaries are excessively rigid or virtually nonexistent. Healthy boundaries flow from a clear sense of self, which the conditioned self struggles to maintain.

Boundary difficulties might look like:

- Saying yes when you want to say no (or vice versa).
- Feeling responsible for others' emotions.
- Difficulty asking for what you need.
- Either walls that keep everyone at arm's length or no limits at all.

These boundary issues reflect conditioned beliefs about your right to have needs, your responsibility for others' wellbeing, and what constitutes acceptable behavior in relationships.

> **"The difference between boundaries and barriers is that boundaries are permeable to the right things." - Henry Cloud.**

Approval-Seeking: The Addiction to Validation

A powerful sign of living from your conditioned self is structuring your behavior around gaining others' approval, even at the expense of your own values or wellbeing.

This approval-seeking might manifest as:

- Making choices based on anticipated reactions from others.
- Excessive apologizing for having needs or opinions.
- Difficulty receiving criticism without shame spirals.
- Constant monitoring of others' responses to you.

The painful cycle of approval-seeking is that it never provides the genuine validation you crave, because the approval isn't for your authentic self but for the persona you're presenting.

Look, we've all been there, right? That little ping of "Did they like me?" after a conversation. But here's the thing: you are already enough. You don't need a chorus of "yeses" to validate your existence. Imagine how freeing it would be to just be, without constantly checking for thumbs-ups. That space, where you're not waiting for someone else's opinion, is where your true power lives. It's where you find the confidence to be yourself, flaws and all, and guess what? That's when people are actually drawn to you – when you're real.

CONDITIONAL SELF-WORTH: THE SHIFTING FOUNDATION

Finally, when living from your conditioned self, your sense of worth tends to fluctuate dramatically based on external circumstances and achievements. This creates a fundamental instability in how you feel about yourself.

Signs of conditional self-worth include:

- Feeling only as good as your last accomplishment.
- Worthiness that depends on others' validation.
- Dramatic mood shifts based on performance or appearance.
- The sense that you must continually earn your right to exist.

This conditional relationship with yourself reflects early experiences where love and acceptance came with conditions, creating the belief that your value must be continually earned rather than being intrinsic.

> **"Conditional love asks for something to give it reason. Unconditional love asks for nothing but to give." - Unknown**

SELF-COMPASSION: THE ESSENTIAL RESPONSE TO THESE SIGNS

Okay, so you're starting to see these patterns, right? The role-playing, the approval-seeking... it can feel a little heavy. But here's the thing: instead of beating yourself up, let's flip the script. This is where compassion comes in. Like, real, deep kindness for yourself. Imagine talking to a friend who's going through this – you wouldn't judge them, you'd offer understanding and support. That's what you deserve too. These patterns, they're not flaws, they're just old survival strategies that aren't serving you anymore. So, let's meet them with gentle curiosity, with a soft "it's okay, I get it." Because when you treat yourself with compassion, you create the space for real change to happen, a space where you can finally start to heal and grow. You're not broken, you're learning, and you're worthy of that kindness.

As you recognize these signs in your own life—and most of us exhibit at least some of them—the most important response is compassion. These patterns developed for good reasons, helping you navigate complex environments with the resources you had available at the time.

In the next section, we'll explore the substantial benefits that come from reconnecting with your authentic self and aligning your emotional life with your deeper truth.

Benefits of Authentic Living and Emotional Alignment

The Rewards of Coming Home to Yourself

After exploring the development of your conditioned patterns and learning to recognize signs of disconnection from your authentic self, you might be wondering: What becomes possible when you begin to align with your true nature? What tangible differences can you expect to experience as you reclaim your emotional authenticity?

The learning path toward authentic living isn't simply about eliminating problems—it's about opening doors to possibilities that may have seemed out of reach. The benefits extend far beyond feeling better (though that certainly happens); they change every dimension of your life in impactful and practical ways.

Psychological and Emotional Benefits: The Inner Transformation

The most immediate changes you'll likely notice as you move toward authentic living occur in your internal perspective—your emotional experience and psychological wellbeing.

Increased Emotional Resilience: Bending Without Breaking

When you're aligned with your authentic self, you develop a remarkable capacity to navigate life's inevitable challenges without being devastated by them. This resilience doesn't mean you won't feel difficult emotions—quite the opposite. It means you can experience the full range of your feelings without being overwhelmed by them.

This resilience manifests as:

- Recovering more quickly from setbacks and disappointments.

- Maintaining perspective during emotional storms.
- Finding meaning in difficult experiences.
- Trusting your capacity to handle whatever comes.

This isn't emotional invulnerability—it's emotional flexibility. Like a tree that bends in strong winds rather than breaking, you learn to move with your emotional experience rather than fighting against it or being uprooted by it.

Reduced Internal Conflict: The Peace of Alignment

One of the most significant benefits of authentic living is the dramatic trimming of internal conflict. When your outward expression aligns with your inner reality, the energy previously spent managing this gap becomes available for living.

Signs of this reduced conflict include:

- Fewer instances of feeling torn between competing needs or values.
- Decreased second-guessing of your decisions.
- Less anxiety about whether you're doing the "right" thing.
- A general sense of being at peace with yourself.

This alignment doesn't mean you'll never face difficult choices or competing priorities. Rather, it means you'll manage these challenges from a clear center rather than from fragmented, conflicting aspects of self.

Expanded Emotional Range: The Full Spectrum of Experience

As you reconnect with your authentic self, you'll likely discover access to a much wider range of emotional experiences. Emotions previously deemed too risky, inappropriate, or overwhelming become available as valuable aspects of your experience.

This expanded range includes:

- Allowing yourself to feel joy without waiting for the other shoe to drop
- Experiencing healthy anger as energy for appropriate boundaries
- Accessing vulnerability and tenderness in close relationships
- Feeling genuine pride in your accomplishments without minimizing them

Many people describe this as "coming back to life" after a period of emotional fatigue or exhaustion. Colors seem brighter, connections feel deeper, and even challenging emotions hold a certain liveliness that makes life feel more real and engaging.

> "Experience is not what happens to you; it's what you do with what happens to you." - Aldous Huxley.

Authentic Happiness: Beyond Toxic Positivity

Perhaps most significantly, authentic living opens the door to a form of happiness fundamentally different from the forced positivity often promoted in our culture. This authentic happiness isn't about maintaining constant good feelings but about experiencing genuine wellbeing that includes the full spectrum of emotions.

Authentic happiness is characterized by:

- Contentment that doesn't depend on circumstances being perfect.
- Appreciation for ordinary moments of connection and beauty.
- A sense of satisfaction independent of external achievements.
- The ability to find joy even amidst life's difficulties.

This form of happiness is sustainable precisely because it doesn't require you to cut off parts of your authentic experience. It flows from wholeness rather than from artificially maintaining positive states.

> "Authentic happiness isn't something we can go out and get, buy, beg, borrow or steal, it's only something we can be, and it's a choice we make with every breath we take." - Dennis Merritt Jones.

Relational Advantages: Authentic Connections

Your relationship with yourself inevitably shapes your relationships with others. As you align with your authentic self, you'll notice significant shifts in how you connect with the people in your life.

Deeper Connections: Beyond Surface-Level Interaction

When you show up authentically, you create the conditions for genuine intimacy with others. The energy previously used to maintain a façade becomes available for real connection.

These deeper connections manifest as:

- Conversations that go beyond small talk to matters of real significance.
- Being known and accepted for who you actually are.
- The ability to be present and attentive with others.
- Relationships characterized by mutual growth rather than mutual performance.

The depth of these connections often surprises people who have spent years operating primarily from their conditioned self. There's a quality of being truly seen and recognized that many find profoundly moving after years of more surface-level interactions.

Attraction of Compatible People: Your Authentic Magnet

An unexpected benefit of authentic living is that you naturally begin to attract relationships that support your true nature while outgrowing those that don't. This isn't about deliberately cutting people off but about a natural evolution as your energy and focus shift.

You may notice:

- New people entering your life who appreciate your authentic qualities.
- Existing relationships either deepening or naturally fading.
- Less time spent on connections that drain your energy.
- A growing circle of people who share your core values.

This natural sorting process isn't about judging others but about aligning with those who can appreciate and support your authentic expression—and whose authentic selves resonate with yours.

Healthy Boundaries: The Foundation of Authentic Connection

As you reclaim your authentic self, you'll develop a clearer sense of where you end and others begin. This natural boundary development protects your wellbeing while allowing for genuine closeness.

Healthy boundaries look like:

- Saying no when you mean no (and yes when you mean yes).
- Taking responsibility for your emotions while letting others own theirs.
- Being able to stay connected to yourself even when others are upset.
- Recognizing and respecting others' boundaries as well.

These boundaries aren't walls that keep others out but clear delineations that actually make deeper connection possible. When both people in a relationship know where they stand, they can meet as whole individuals rather than as entangled parts.

Conflict Transformation: From Reactivity to Response

Perhaps one of the most valuable relational benefits is a transformed relationship with conflict. Rather than avoiding conflicts at all costs or being consumed by them, you develop the capacity to use disagreements as opportunities for deeper understanding.

This transformation might look like:

- Staying present during difficult conversations rather than shutting down or exploding.
- Curiosity about differences instead of needing everyone to agree with you.
- The ability to hear criticism without collapsing into shame or defensiveness.
- Finding creative solutions that honor everyone's authentic needs.

Conflicts become opportunities to know yourself and others more deeply rather than threats to emotional safety or relationship stability.

> **"Respond intelligently even to unintelligent treatment." - Lao Tzu.**

Life Direction and Purpose: Alignment in Action

Beyond internal and relational benefits, authentic living transforms how you travel your life path and make meaningful choices.

Aligned Decision-Making: Clarity in Choices

One of the most practical benefits of reconnecting with your authentic self is greater ease in decision-making. When you have access to your genuine preferences and values, choices become clearer.

This aligned decision-making manifests as:

- Confidence in your choices without excessive second-guessing.
- Decisions that consider both practical realities and emotional wisdom.
- The ability to say no to opportunities that don't align with your values.
- Choices that reflect who you are rather than who you think you should be.

This doesn't mean decisions are always easy or that you'll never feel conflicted. But the nature of the decision-making process shifts from anxious contemplation to thoughtful discernment.

Natural Motivation: Energy for What Matters

When your actions align with your authentic self, you access a form of motivation fundamentally different from the driven, should-based energy of conditioning. This natural motivation feels like being pulled toward what matters rather than pushing yourself to perform.

Signs of this natural motivation include:

- Finding energy for activities that previously seemed draining

- Needing less external reward or recognition to stay engaged
- Recovery that happens through engagement rather than escape
- The ability to persist through difficulties because the purpose matters to you

This shift from extrinsic to intrinsic motivation creates sustainable energy for long-term projects and commitments. You're no longer running on the finite fuel of approval or achievement but on the renewable energy of alignment with what genuinely matters to you.

Meaningful Contribution: Your Unique Offering

As you live more authentically, you naturally begin to make contributions that reflect your unique combination of gifts, experiences, and perspectives. Rather than trying to fit your offering into predetermined boxes, you find ways to contribute that feel genuinely yours.

This might look like:

- Work that utilizes your natural strengths rather than just your trained skills.
- Creative expression that has your distinctive signature.
- Service that addresses needs you genuinely care about.
- Leadership that reflects your authentic values and vision.

These contributions tend to have a different quality than those made from conditioning alone—they carry a vitality and originality that comes from their authentic source.

> **"What you do makes a difference, and you have to decide what kind of difference you want to make." - Jane Goodall.**

Values-Based Living: Your Personal North Star

Perhaps the most significant aspect of authentic living is that your daily choices become increasingly guided by what truly matters to you rather than by external pressures or conditioned shoulds.

Values-based living manifests as:

- Consistency between your stated priorities and how you actually spend your time and energy.
- Decisions that reflect your core values even when they're challenging.
- The ability to stay true to what matters amid external pressures.
- A sense of integrity between your internal compass and outer actions.

This alignment creates a unified narrative to your life—not because you're following a predetermined script, but because your choices flow from a consistent center.

Research-Backed Outcomes: The Science of Authenticity

While the benefits of authentic living might sound idealistic, they're actually grounded in a substantial body of research. Studies across multiple disciplines consistently find that authentic living correlates with significant improvements in wellbeing and functioning.

Health and Longevity: Your Body on Authenticity

Research in psychoneuroimmunology—the study of how psychological factors affect physical health—reveals that emotional authenticity has measurable effects on physical wellbeing:

- Reduced inflammation markers associated with chronic disease.
- Improved immune system functioning.
- Better cardiovascular health outcomes.
- Even potential impacts on cellular aging processes.

These findings make sense when you consider the physiological strain of chronic inauthenticity. Your body registers the gap between your inner reality and outer presentation as a form of threat, triggering stress responses that, over time, create wear and tear on multiple body systems.

Stress Reduction: The Relief of Congruence

One of the most well-documented benefits of authentic living is a significant reduction in perceived stress and its physiological markers:

- Lower cortisol levels (the primary stress hormone).
- Decreased muscle tension and related pain.
- Improved sleep quality and duration.
- Better recovery from stressful events.

This stress reduction isn't about avoiding challenging situations but about approaching them with internal coherence rather than fragmentation. When you're not fighting against yourself, you have more resources available to meet external challenges.

> **"The greatest weapon against stress is our ability to choose one thought over another." - William James.**

Cognitive Benefits: Your Brain on Authenticity

Cognitive research demonstrates that authentic living enhances mental functioning in several important ways:

- Improved focus and attention through reduced internal conflict.
- Enhanced creative problem-solving through access to intuitive processes.
- Better decision-making with fewer decision fatigue effects.
- Increased cognitive flexibility and adaptation to new information.

These cognitive benefits likely stem from the reduced cognitive load when you're not constantly monitoring, editing, and censoring your authentic responses. With less energy devoted to impression management, more mental resources are available for present-moment engagement and clear thinking.

> **"Good decisions come from experience, and experience comes from bad decisions." - Mark Twain.**

Life Satisfaction: The Research on Happiness

Finally, a substantial body of research in positive psychology consistently links authenticity with higher levels of subjective wellbeing and life satisfaction:

- Greater overall happiness and life satisfaction.
- More frequent experiences of flow and engagement.
- Higher scores on measures of psychological wellbeing.
- Increased resilience during life transitions and challenges.

These findings cut across demographic differences, suggesting that authentic living contributes to wellbeing regardless of specific life circumstances or cultural contexts.

The Path Forward: From Understanding to Action

Okay, so we've talked a lot about understanding, right? Seeing those patterns, recognizing those triggers. But knowing isn't the same as doing. It's like, you can read all the books about riding a bike, but you gotta actually get on and pedal, right? This is where the action comes in. It's about taking those insights and turning them into real-life changes. It's about choosing courage over comfort, about stepping outside those old familiar roles and trying something new. It's not gonna be perfect, there will be stumbles, but every small step, every conscious choice to be more authentic, it builds momentum. It's like you're rewiring your brain, creating new pathways. So, let's take that understanding and start moving. Let's start living those changes, one brave step at a time.

The benefits of authentic living aren't distant possibilities but natural outcomes of the alignment process. Each step toward greater authenticity—however small—brings corresponding increases in wellbeing, connection, and purpose.

As we conclude this chapter on understanding the distinction between your authentic and conditioned selves, you now have a framework for recognizing patterns that may have been invisible to you before. This awareness is the essential foundation for the practical work of emotional alignment that follows in the rest of this book.

In the next chapter, we'll explore the alignment process itself—how to bridge the gap between where you are now and a more authentic relationship with your emotions and self. You'll learn practical strategies for reconnecting with your authentic self while honoring the protective intentions of your conditioned patterns.

Remember, the journey toward authenticity isn't about achieving a perfect state of being but about moving progressively toward greater congruence between your inner reality and outer expression. Each moment of alignment is complete in itself—not just a step toward a future goal but an experience of wholeness available right now.

Chapter 3: The Alignment Process

You've felt the disconnect. That jarring moment when what you're doing and saying doesn't match what you're actually feeling. The exhaustion that follows a day of performing rather than being. The silent resignation as you once again set aside your authentic response for one that feels safer, more acceptable, or simply more familiar.

This gap between your authentic self and your lived experience isn't just uncomfortable—it's costly. It drains your energy, strains your relationships, and creates a persistent sense that something essential is missing from your life, even when everything looks fine on the surface.

The good news? This gap isn't fixed or permanent. It can be bridged, not through dramatic upheaval or perfect authenticity in every moment, but through a practical process of alignment that gradually brings your outer expression into harmony with your inner truth.

Think of it like this: If Chapter 2 helped you recognize the two distinct tracks of your experience—your authentic self and your conditioned patterns—Chapter 3 is about bringing those tracks closer together. It's about creating integration where there has been division, congruence where there has been contradiction.

This alignment process isn't about achieving some perfect state of perpetual authenticity. That's not how being human works. Rather, it's about developing the capacity to notice when you've drifted from your authentic center and the skills to find your way back. It's about turning alignment from an occasional accident into a consistent practice.

In the pages ahead, we'll explore both the obstacles that maintain misalignment and the specific stages of the return journey to authenticity. You'll learn practical approaches for creating the safety that makes authentic exploration possible, even in challenging circumstances.

Some of this territory may feel uncomfortable at first. After all, there were good reasons you developed patterns of disconnection—they served important protective functions in your past. Approaching these patterns with compassion rather than criticism creates the conditions where authentic alignment becomes possible.

The Misalignment Between Emotions and True Self

Understanding the Gap That Causes Suffering

Now that you understand the distinction between your authentic and conditioned selves, let's explore what happens when a gap develops between your emotional truth and your lived experience. This misalignment—the disconnect between what you truly feel and what you allow yourself to express or even acknowledge—lies at the heart of emotional suffering.

Imagine two tracks of a railway gradually diverging. One track represents your authentic emotional experience—the natural responses arising from your true self. The other represents your expressed or acknowledged emotions—what you permit yourself to feel and show. The further these tracks separate, the greater the strain on your entire system.

What Emotional Misalignment Feels Like

You've likely experienced emotional misalignment many times, perhaps without having a name for it. It's that unsettled feeling when you're smiling at a party while inwardly counting the minutes until you can leave. It's the heaviness in your chest when you say "I'm fine" while something important remains unaddressed. It's the tension that builds when you pursue goals that look impressive but don't resonate with what truly matters to you.

Misalignment manifests in numerous ways:

- A persistent sense that something is "off" or "not right".
- Feeling like you're playing a role rather than living authentically.
- Physical tension or discomfort that doesn't have a clear cause.
- Emotional numbness or disconnection from your experiences.
- A gap between your public persona and private reality.
- Exhaustion that rest alone doesn't seem to remedy.

These experiences exist along a spectrum. At one end is minor incongruence—small moments where you briefly override your authentic response. At the other end is profound disconnection—a pervasive sense of estrangement from your true emotional life.

You might recognize misalignment in everyday scenarios like these:

- Laughing at a joke that actually offends you.
- Agreeing to commitments that you inwardly resist.
- Suppressing anger or hurt to maintain harmony.
- Pursuing achievements that don't bring genuine satisfaction.
- Staying in situations that drain you while insisting you're happy.

Each of these moments might seem inconsequential in isolation. But collectively, they create a pattern of divided attention—part of you engaged in what's happening, another part monitoring and managing your authentic responses. This division consumes enormous energy and disconnects you from the wisdom of your emotional guidance system.

How the Emotional Gap Develops

This misalignment doesn't happen overnight. It develops gradually through thousands of interactions where your authentic emotional responses were met with disapproval, dismissal, or even danger.

As a child, your emotional expression was largely shaped by your caregivers' responses. If your tears were consistently met with "Don't be a baby," you learned to suppress sadness. If your anger triggered punishment, you learned to hide that too. If your enthusiasm was labeled as "too much," you learned to dampen your joy.

These early adaptations were brilliantly protective. When your survival and sense of belonging depended on the adults around you, conforming to their emotional expectations was a necessary adaptation. The problem isn't that you developed these patterns—it's that they've outlived their usefulness while remaining largely unconscious.

As you grew, these patterns became increasingly automatic. Each time you overrode an authentic response, the pathway to disconnection becomes more established in your neural circuitry. What began as conscious effort ("I shouldn't cry here") eventually became automatic emotional filtering that happens outside your awareness.

Significant difficult experiences can dramatically widen this gap. When emotions are too overwhelming or dangerous to process—as in traumatic events—your system protects you through various forms of disconnection. While this disconnection serves as immediate protection, it often persists long after the threat has passed, creating a fortress that keeps out both pain and joy.

The Costs of Sustained Misalignment

Living with chronic misalignment between your authentic emotions and your conscious experience extracts a steep price across every dimension of your wellbeing.

Physical Costs

Your body bears the burden of emotional incongruence. When you consistently override authentic responses, your physiology registers this as a form of threat, triggering stress responses that were designed for short-term emergencies, not chronic conditions:

- Persistent muscle tension, particularly in the jaw, neck, and shoulders.
- Compromised immune function and increased inflammation.
- Disrupted sleep patterns and reduced restoration.
- Digestive disturbances reflecting the gut-brain connection.
- Lowered energy as resources are diverted to managing internal conflict.

Your body keeps the score of emotional misalignment, creating physical symptoms that often seem mysterious until you recognize their emotional roots.

Psychological Costs

Psychologically, misalignment creates a state of internal division that undermines wellbeing in numerous ways:

- Anxiety that emerges from the constant vigilance of self-monitoring.
- Depression that reflects the loss of connection to your authentic experience.
- Confusion about your own wants, needs, and preferences.
- Diminished access to intuition and internal guidance.
- Increased vulnerability to external pressure and manipulation.

Perhaps most significantly, sustained misalignment creates a painful sense of falseness—the nagging feeling that you're somehow living inauthentically even if others see you as successful.

"Balance is not something you find, it's something you create." - Jana Kingsford.

Relational Costs

Your relationships inevitably reflect your relationship with yourself. When you're disconnected from your authentic emotions, your connections with others suffer in parallel ways:

- Surface-level interactions that never reach genuine intimacy.
- Recurring misunderstandings as your true feelings remain hidden.
- Resentment that builds when authentic needs go unexpressed.
- Attraction to relationships that reinforce familiar patterns of disconnection.
- The painful paradox of feeling lonely even when surrounded by others.

True connection requires emotional authenticity. When you're misaligned with your own emotions, others relate to your presentation rather than your authentic self, creating interactions that never satisfy your deeper longing for being known and accepted.

Spiritual Costs

Beyond the physical, psychological, and relational impacts, emotional misalignment disconnects you from deeper dimensions of existence:

- Separation from your sense of meaning and purpose.
- Difficulty accessing intuitive wisdom and guidance.
- Disconnection from what you truly value and hold sacred.
- The existential emptiness that comes from living someone else's life.
- Loss of the awe, wonder, and gratitude that emerge from authentic presence.

While these spiritual costs may seem less tangible than others, many people report them as the most painful aspect of misalignment—the sense that life is passing by without being truly lived.

"True discomfort comes from being out of alignment with your true self. Everything else is just an obstacle to overcome." - Panache Desai.

WHY ALIGNMENT MATTERS: YOUR NATURAL STATE

You know that feeling when everything just clicks? Like you're in your groove, doing what you're meant to be doing? That's your natural state, it's just you being you, without all the extra baggage.

The importance of emotional alignment isn't based on some abstract ideal but on a fundamental reality of human functioning: your system naturally seeks coherence. Integration—the harmonious connection between different aspects of your experience—is your birthright and your biological imperative.

From a neurobiological perspective, alignment between your emotional experience and conscious awareness creates integration between different brain regions. The embodied emotions processed by your limbic system and the executive functions of your prefrontal cortex work as partners rather than adversaries, creating a state of neural harmony that supports optimal functioning.

Relationally, alignment enables authentic connection. When you're present with your own experience, you can be present with others, creating the conditions for genuine intimacy and understanding rather than the performance of social roles.

The world needs you in that state. It needs your unique energy, your specific gifts. All those masks we wear, all those roles we play, they dim our light. When you drop them, when you align, you shine brighter, and you inspire others to do the same. It's like, you're not just doing yourself a favor, you're doing the world a favor. You're showing up as the real you, and that's a powerful thing.

The journey toward alignment isn't about reaching some perfect state—it's about progressively reducing the gap between your authentic emotional experience and what you acknowledge and express. Each step in this direction brings immediate benefits in wellbeing, connection, and vitality.

> **"When the way you think, speak and behave match your values, life feels very good. You feel whole, content, in control. But when these do not align, things feel... wrong. Life feels uneasy. You feel out of touch, discontented, restless, confused." - Cheryl Richardson.**

Your authentic self has never actually disappeared, even during your most disconnected moments. It has always remained present, patiently waiting beneath the layers of conditioning and protection. The journey ahead isn't about creating something new but about returning to what has always been there—your natural state of emotional wholeness and authenticity.

Common Barriers to Emotional Authenticity

Getting to that authentic place isn't always a walk in the park. We all have those little battles in our heads, right? Fear of judgment, that's a big one. We worry what people will think if we drop the act, if we show our "real" selves. And then there's the whole "comfort zone" thing. It's cozy in those old patterns, even if they're not great for us. Change is scary, and our brains are wired to avoid it. Plus, sometimes we're just plain exhausted. Dealing with life is draining, and it feels easier to just keep doing what we've always done.

Understanding What Stands in Your Way

Getting to that place of emotional alignment? It's not a straight path. You'll run into obstacles, things that slow you down or even stop you for a bit. But understanding what those things are? That's key. It helps you realize, "Hey, I'm not the only one." These aren't signs of failure, they're just part of being human.

Like any meaningful journey, it includes obstacles that can slow your progress or temporarily block your way forward. Understanding these common barriers doesn't just prepare you for the challenges ahead—it normalizes the struggles you've likely already experienced in your attempts to live more authentically. And when you can see them clearly, you can learn to work with them, to keep moving forward.

Fear-Based Barriers: The Protective Warnings

At the most fundamental level, many barriers to emotional authenticity are rooted in fear—not irrational fear, but intelligent protective responses based on past experiences. Your system has learned what felt dangerous before and works diligently to prevent similar pain in the future.

Fear of Rejection: The Social Survival Threat

Perhaps the most powerful fear-based barrier is the deeply wired concern that authentic emotional expression will lead to rejection or abandonment. This fear isn't simply psychological—it's biological. Your brain evolved in an environment where social rejection could literally mean death, as survival depended on being part of a group.

This fear manifests in thoughts like:

- "If people knew how I really felt, they wouldn't accept me."
- "My true emotions are too much for others to handle."
- "I need to keep these feelings hidden to maintain my relationships."
- "Being myself means being alone."

The pain of this fear is both anticipatory (dreading potential rejection) and reinforcing (when authentic expressions have led to actual rejection). It creates a powerful incentive to hide your true feelings behind acceptable presentations.

What makes this barrier particularly challenging is that it's sometimes validated by experience. There are environments and relationships where authentic expression does lead to rejection. The key is distinguishing between contexts where this fear is describing current reality versus contexts where it's replaying past wounds.

Fear of Overwhelm: The Emotional Flood Warning

Another common barrier is the fear that fully experiencing your authentic emotions will be overwhelming—that you'll be swept away by feelings too powerful to contain or navigate. This fear often emerges from early experiences where you lacked support for processing intense emotions.

This manifests in thoughts such as:

- "If I start crying, I might never stop."
- "My anger scares me—I don't know what I might do."
- "These feelings are too big for me to handle."
- "I'll lose control if I really let myself feel this."

The anticipatory anxiety of this fear often creates a self-fulfilling prophecy. When emotions are only allowed expression after building to extreme intensity, they do indeed feel overwhelming when finally released. This reinforces the belief that emotions themselves are dangerous, when the real issue is the delayed recognition and expression.

Fear of Responsibility: The Burden of Knowledge

A more subtle fear-based barrier is the concern about what emotional authenticity might require of you. Acknowledging your true feelings often reveals inconvenient truths about your life that might demand significant changes.

This fear sounds like:

- "If I admit how unhappy I am, I might have to leave this relationship/job"
- "Recognizing these feelings would mean admitting I've been on the wrong path"
- "If I acknowledge what I really want, I'll have to face how far I am from having it"
- "Being authentic might mean disappointing people who count on me"

This fear accurately recognizes that emotional authenticity isn't just an internal shift—it eventually reshapes your external choices and relationships. What it doesn't account for is the cost of continuing to live in misalignment, which ultimately extracts a higher price than the changes authenticity might require.

FEAR OF CHANGE: THE UNKNOWN TERRITORY

Finally, there's the fundamental human resistance to venturing into unfamiliar territory. Your conditioned patterns, even when painful, have the advantage of being known. Emotional authenticity represents uncharted waters.

This barrier speaks through thoughts like:

- "What if I don't like who I really am?"
- "My current struggles are at least familiar—what new problems will emerge?"
- "I've built my life around being this way—who would I be otherwise?"
- "What if authentic living is just another disappointment?"

This fear reveals the profound identity questions that authentic living eventually raises. The journey isn't just about emotional expression but about who you understand yourself to be at the most fundamental level.

> **"Fear is the brain's way of saying that there is something important for you to overcome." - Rachel Huber.**

SKILL-BASED BARRIERS: THE MISSING TOOLS

Beyond fears, many barriers to emotional authenticity involve underdeveloped skills. These aren't innate deficiencies but simply capacities that weren't nurtured in your particular developmental environment.

EMOTIONAL LITERACY: THE LANGUAGE OF FEELING

One of the most common skill barriers is limited emotional vocabulary and recognition—what psychologists call alexithymia, or difficulty identifying and describing emotions. Without words to name your experiences, emotions remain vague, confusing signals rather than specific, useful information.

Signs of this barrier include:

- Describing most emotions as simply "good" or "bad".
- Recognizing emotions only at extreme intensity.
- Difficulty distinguishing between similar emotions (like shame and guilt).
- Better recognition of others' emotions than your own.

This barrier often results from growing up in environments where emotional language was limited or where emotions were treated as problems rather than information. The good news is that emotional literacy can be developed at any age through deliberate practice and attention.

ATTENTIONAL CHALLENGES: THE WANDERING MIND

Another common skill barrier involves difficulty sustaining attention to internal experience. In a culture filled with external stimulation and distractions, the capacity to maintain awareness of subtle internal signals often remains underdeveloped.

This manifests as:

- Mind wandering during attempts at self-reflection.
- Distractibility during emotional conversations.
- Difficulty staying with uncomfortable feelings.
- The habit of intellectualizing rather than experiencing emotions.

This barrier reflects both cultural conditioning that prioritizes external focus and potential discomfort with internal attention. Developing the capacity to maintain present-moment awareness of your emotional experience is a foundational skill that supports all aspects of authentic living.

REGULATION DEFICITS: THE MISSING MIDDLE GEAR

Many people struggle with emotional authenticity because they lack experience with the middle ground between suppression and overwhelming expression. Without regulation skills, emotions seem to have only two settings: completely off or completely overwhelming.

Signs of regulation challenges include:

- Feeling that emotions are either hidden or out of control.
- "Emotional leakage" where suppressed feelings emerge indirectly.
- Avoiding certain emotions because you don't know how to navigate them.
- Relying on external regulation (substances, people, activities) to manage feelings.

This barrier often stems from missing out on what developmental psychologists call "emotion coaching"—adult guidance in navigating feelings during childhood. Without this modeling, you may have never learned that emotions can be fully felt while still being skillfully contained and expressed.

INTEGRATION OBSTACLES: THE MEANING-MAKING CHALLENGE

The final skill barrier involves difficulty integrating emotional experiences into a coherent narrative and meaning system. Without this integration, emotions remain isolated events rather than connected aspects of your unfolding life story.

This shows up as:

- Compartmentalizing different emotional experiences.
- Difficulty seeing patterns in your emotional responses.
- Disconnection between emotional knowledge and practical decisions.
- Struggle to extract meaning and growth from difficult feelings.

Integration requires the capacity to step back from immediate experience and recognize the larger patterns and meanings at work. Without this skill, authentic emotions may be felt but not fully utilized for their guidance and growth potential.

Environmental Barriers: The External Constraints

Beyond internal fears and skill gaps, external circumstances can create very real barriers to emotional authenticity.

Unsupportive Relationships: The Discouraging Context

Perhaps the most significant environmental barrier is being embedded in relationships that actively discourage authentic expression. These might be family systems, work environments, or social circles where conformity is valued over authenticity.

This looks like:

- Relationships where certain emotions are explicitly or implicitly forbidden.
- Social contexts where vulnerability is exploited rather than honored.
- Workplaces that require emotional performances disconnected from authenticity.
- Communities with rigid expectations about appropriate emotional expression.

While internal work can help you maintain connection to your authentic self even in challenging environments, there are genuinely toxic contexts where full authenticity might not be safe or possible. Discernment about where, when, and how to express your authentic emotions is an important aspect of emotional intelligence.

Practical Demands: The Time and Energy Constraints

Another environmental barrier involves the practical limitations of modern life. Authentic living requires time for reflection, processing, and integration—resources that may be scarce in demanding circumstances.

This barrier manifests as:

- Work schedules that leave little time for emotional processing.
- Caretaking responsibilities that prioritize others' needs.
- Financial pressures that necessitate emotionally incongruent choices.
- Physical exhaustion that limits capacity for internal attention.

These practical constraints are very real and often reflect systemic issues beyond individual control. Finding ways to create even small spaces for authentic connection within these constraints becomes an important practice in itself.

Cultural Messaging: The Collective Devaluing

Broader cultural attitudes toward emotions can create powerful barriers to authenticity. Many societies explicitly or implicitly dismiss emotional intelligence as less valuable than other forms of capability.

This shows up as:

- Messages that emotions are "soft" or less important than logic
- Gendered attitudes about acceptable emotional expression
- Media portrayal of emotional authenticity as weakness
- Educational systems that prioritize academic over emotional development

These cultural messages create an unsupportive background for your personal journey toward authenticity. Recognizing their influence allows you to consciously evaluate rather than unconsciously absorb these perspectives.

> **"You may encounter many defeats, but you must not be defeated. In fact, it may be necessary to encounter the defeats, so you can know who you are, what you can rise from, how you can still come out of it." - Maya Angelou.**

Technological Distractions: The Modern Disconnection

A uniquely modern environmental barrier involves the constant availability of technological distractions that pull attention away from internal experience.

Signs of this barrier include:

- Reflexively checking devices during moments of emotional discomfort
- Substituting virtual connection for emotional presence
- Information overload that overwhelms capacity for reflection
- Shortened attention spans that make emotional awareness difficult

These technologies aren't inherently problematic, but their design often explicitly aims to capture and hold attention that might otherwise be available for internal awareness and authentic connection.

> **"By prevailing over all obstacles and distractions, one may unfailingly arrive at his chosen goal or destination."** - Christopher Columbus.

Internal Belief Barriers: The Limiting Mindsets

The final category of barriers involves internal beliefs about emotions and authenticity that limit your progress even when you consciously value authentic living.

Perfectionism: The Impossible Standard

One common belief barrier is perfectionism applied to emotional life—the idea that authentic living means never struggling, never falling into old patterns, and always knowing exactly what you feel.

This manifests as thoughts like:

- "I should be better at this by now."
- "Real emotional intelligence would mean never getting triggered."
- "If I were truly authentic, I wouldn't have these doubts."
- "Others seem to have this figured out already."

This perfectionism creates a standard that no human can meet, turning the journey toward authenticity into another arena for self-judgment rather than self-discovery.

All-or-Nothing Thinking: The False Dichotomy

Another limiting belief is the idea that authenticity is an absolute state rather than a direction and ongoing practice. This creates a false dichotomy where you're either completely authentic or completely inauthentic.

This shows up in thoughts such as:

- "I was being totally fake in that situation."
- "If I'm not expressing every feeling, I'm being inauthentic."
- "I can't be partially authentic—it's all or nothing."
- "If I were truly authentic, I would never adjust my expression for context."

This binary thinking misses the nuanced reality that authenticity exists on a spectrum and varies across contexts. It's not about perfection but about increasing alignment over time.

Emotional Hierarchies: The Value Judgment

Many people unconsciously maintain hierarchies of emotions, seeing some feelings as inherently better, more spiritual, or more evolved than others. This creates barriers to accepting the full range of authentic experience.

This belief system sounds like:

- "Spiritual people don't get angry."
- "Negative emotions show I'm not growing."
- "I should be beyond feeling hurt by now."
- "Authentic people are always compassionate/peaceful/loving"

These hierarchies create internal conflict when your authentic experience includes emotions you've judged as less worthy or evolved. True emotional authenticity embraces the full spectrum of human feeling without these value judgments.

> **"You begin to fly when you let go of self-limiting beliefs and allow your mind and aspirations to rise to greater heights." - Brian Tracy.**

Progress Myths: The Linear Illusion

Finally, many people hold beliefs about personal growth as a linear, continuous upward progression. This creates expectations that clash with the cyclical, sometimes messy reality of emotional development.

This appears in thoughts like:

- "I've worked through this already—I shouldn't be facing it again."
- "True healing would mean never returning to these feelings."
- "I'm back at square one if these patterns reemerge."
- "Growth should feel good and affirming all the time."

These beliefs fail to recognize that emotional development typically moves in spirals rather than straight lines, revisiting similar themes at deeper levels over time.

Working With Barriers: The Path Through

Recognizing these common barriers isn't cause for discouragement but for compassionate understanding of the complex factors that influence your journey toward authenticity. Each barrier you identify represents not an obstacle but an opportunity—a specific area where targeted attention and practice can create significant shifts.

In the sections that follow, we'll explore the practical process of alignment that allows you to work skillfully with these barriers rather than being stopped by them. Remember that every person walking a path of emotional authenticity encounters these challenges in some form. What differentiates those who progress isn't the absence of barriers but the willingness to engage with them as part of the journey itself.

The Four Stages of Emotional Alignment

The Path from Disconnection to Integration

Now that you understand the common barriers to emotional authenticity, let's explore the practical process of bridging the gap between your conditioned patterns and your authentic emotional experience. This alignment process isn't a single event but a sequence of stages that unfolds gradually as you move toward greater congruence between your inner truth and outer expression.

Think of these stages as a natural progression—each building upon the previous one while creating the foundation for what follows. While I've organized them sequentially for clarity, in practice you may find yourself moving back and forth between stages or working with different emotions at different stages simultaneously. The process is less like climbing a staircase and more like a spiral, revisiting similar territory at progressively deeper levels.

Let's examine each stage of this transformative journey.

Stage 1: Awareness - Recognizing Misalignment

The alignment process begins with a simple yet profound shift: noticing the gap between your authentic emotional experience and what you're acknowledging or expressing. This awareness is the essential first step without which no further movement is possible.

How Awareness Emerges

Awareness of emotional misalignment typically emerges in one of several ways:

- **Through discomfort** — Physical tension, anxiety, or a vague sense of wrongness signals that something is off between your inner experience and outer reality.
- **Through patterns** — Recognizing recurring situations where you feel inauthentic or emotionally disconnected reveals habitual misalignments.
- **Through contrast** — Experiencing rare moments of deep authenticity highlights the misalignment present in your everyday life by comparison.

- **Through reflection** — Deliberate contemplation of your emotional life reveals gaps you may have been unconsciously maintaining.
- **Through feedback** — Sometimes others notice your incongruence before you do, offering a mirror that can initiate awareness.

Regardless of how it begins, this awakening to misalignment often feels simultaneously uncomfortable and liberating—uncomfortable because it challenges the status quo, liberating because it names a truth you've likely sensed but not fully acknowledged.

The Quality of Attention

Not all awareness is created equal. The quality of attention you bring to noticing misalignment significantly influences how this stage unfolds. Consider these different qualities of awareness:

- Judgmental awareness notices misalignment with criticism and self-blame: "I can't believe I'm still doing this. What's wrong with me?"
- Analytical awareness intellectualizes the observation: "Interesting how I display different emotions than I'm feeling."
- Compassionate awareness brings kindness to the recognition: "I see how I've learned to hide these feelings to protect myself."

While any form of awareness can initiate the alignment process, compassionate awareness creates the safest conditions for deeper exploration. It acknowledges misalignment as an intelligent adaptation rather than a personal failing.

Common Obstacles to Awareness

Several factors commonly interfere with this crucial first stage:

- **Busyness** — A packed schedule with minimal downtime leaves little space for noticing subtle internal signals.
- **Distraction** — External stimulation (especially digital) continuously pulls attention away from internal experience.
- **Emotional Blindness** — Limited emotional vocabulary makes it difficult to recognize and name what you're feeling.
- **Habitual numbing** — Regular use of substances or behaviors that dampen emotional awareness maintains disconnection.
- **Fear of what you'll find** — Unconscious concern that awareness will require uncomfortable change can actually prevent recognition.

These obstacles aren't insurmountable but do require intentional practices to overcome.

PRACTICES FOR DEVELOPING AWARENESS

You can cultivate greater awareness of emotional misalignment through several approaches:

- **Regular check-ins** — Pausing several times daily to ask, "What am I feeling right now?" creates windows for recognition.
- **Body scanning** — Systematically bringing attention to physical sensations reveals emotional information stored in the body.
- **Emotion journaling** — Writing about your emotional experiences helps identify patterns of misalignment.
- **Mindfulness practice** — Formal meditation develops the attentional muscle that supports emotional awareness.
- **Feedback invitation** — Asking trusted others to reflect back incongruence they notice provides valuable external perspective.

These practices don't need to be time-consuming—even brief moments of intentional awareness create openings for recognition. The key is consistency rather than duration, gradually building your capacity to notice misalignment as it occurs.

As awareness develops, you'll likely discover both longstanding patterns of misalignment and moment-to-moment gaps between authentic experience and expression. Each recognition is valuable, whether it reveals a lifelong pattern or a momentary disconnect.

STAGE 2: ACCEPTANCE - ALLOWING WHAT IS

Once you've recognized misalignment, the next stage involves a profound yet often challenging shift: accepting the reality of your current situation without immediate attempts to fix or change it. This acceptance creates the psychological safety necessary for deeper exploration.

THE TRUE NATURE OF ACCEPTANCE

Acceptance is perhaps the most misunderstood stage of the alignment process. It doesn't mean resignation, approval, or giving up on change. Rather, it means acknowledging what is actually happening right now without resistance or premature problem-solving.

True acceptance involves:

- Acknowledging your authentic feelings, even when they're uncomfortable.
- Recognizing the protective purpose behind your conditioned patterns.

- Allowing both your authentic emotions and your conditioned responses to exist without trying to immediately change either.
- Meeting your current experience with compassion rather than judgment.

This acceptance creates a foundation of inner safety that paradoxically makes change possible. When parts of your experience no longer need to defend themselves against rejection, they can gradually reveal their deeper needs and wisdom.

The Paradox of Change

One of the most powerful insights in emotional work is what psychologists call "the paradox of change"—the principle that we can only truly change what we first accept. This paradox reveals itself consistently in the alignment process:

- Accepting your anger allows it to reveal the boundary violation beneath it.
- Accepting your people-pleasing pattern reveals the legitimate need for connection it serves.
- Accepting your emotional numbness honors the protective function it provides.
- Accepting your fear allows you to respond to it with wisdom rather than reaction.

Change that emerges from acceptance has a different quality than change forced through willpower or self-criticism. It arises naturally as your system recognizes safer ways to meet the needs that your misalignment has been addressing in the best way it knew how.

Common Resistance Patterns

Acceptance often triggers immediate resistance, as it challenges our cultural conditioning toward quick fixes and problem-solving. Common resistance patterns include:

- **Premature action** — Jumping immediately to "how do I fix this?" without fully acknowledging what's happening.
- **Self-criticism** — Judging yourself for having the misalignment in the first place.
- **Rationalization** — Explaining away the misalignment with logical justifications.
- **Minimization** — Downplaying the significance of the gap between authentic and expressed emotions.
- **Future focus** — Constantly emphasizing how things will be different later without fully meeting the current reality.

These resistance patterns aren't character flaws but natural protective responses. Recognizing them with compassion rather than judgment helps gradually dissolve them.

The Physiology of Acceptance

Acceptance isn't just a mental attitude but a whole-body experience. When you truly accept your current reality—including both your authentic emotions and your conditioned patterns—your physiology shifts in measurable ways:

- Muscle tension decreases.
- Breathing becomes deeper and more regular.
- Heart rate variability increases (a measure of nervous system flexibility).
- Stress hormones like cortisol decrease.
- Neural integration between emotional and cognitive centers increases.

These physiological changes create optimal conditions for the exploration and integration that follows. Your body recognizes acceptance as safety, allowing defensive postures to relax.

> "Acceptance doesn't mean resignation; it means understanding that something is what it is and that there's got to be a way through it." - Michael J. Fox.

PRACTICES FOR CULTIVATING ACCEPTANCE

Several approaches can help develop your capacity for genuine acceptance:

- **Self-compassion practices** — Actively offering yourself the same kindness you would offer a friend facing similar challenges.
- **Mindful acknowledgment** — Simply naming your experience without judgment: "This is anger," "This is my people-pleasing pattern".
- **Physical grounding** — Using body-centered practices like deep breathing or feeling your feet on the ground to create a sense of safety.
- **Acceptance language** — Replacing phrases like "I shouldn't feel this way" with "This is what I'm feeling right now".
- **The guest house approach** — Imagining each emotion and pattern as a visitor to be welcomed rather than an intruder to be expelled.

These practices gradually expand your capacity to hold your full experience with compassion, creating the container within which authentic alignment becomes possible.

Alright, let's talk about building that acceptance muscle, because it's a game-changer. Think of it like this: you're creating a safe space within yourself, a place where all parts of you are welcome. And here's how we do it:

First, let's start with self-compassion. Imagine a family member is struggling, what would you say? Now, say that to yourself. Be kind, be gentle. Then, mindful acknowledgment – just naming what's happening, no judgment, like, "Okay, this is anxiety, I can see you." It's like shining a light, bringing awareness. And when things feel overwhelming, ground yourself. Feel your feet, breathe deep. It's about bringing your body into the moment, creating a sense of safety.

> **"The first step toward change is awareness. The second step is acceptance." - Nathaniel Branden.**

Stage 3: Attunement - Reconnecting with Authentic Emotions

With awareness and acceptance established, the third stage involves actively reconnecting with your authentic emotional experience beneath conditioned patterns. This attunement is about listening deeply to the emotional messages you've been missing or misinterpreting.

The Listening Process

Attunement requires a particular quality of internal listening—not analytical problem-solving but receptive presence. This listening involves:

- Bringing curious attention to your emotional experience.
- Creating space for feelings to unfold at their own pace.
- Noticing the information contained within emotions.
- Listening for the needs and values your emotions are highlighting.

This listening happens best in a state of relaxed alertness—neither grasping for insights nor passively disconnected, but receptively present with what emerges.

Somatic Awareness: The Body's Wisdom

Your body offers one of the most direct pathways to authentic emotional reconnection. Emotions always manifest physically before they register cognitively, making somatic awareness a powerful tool for attunement.

Approaches to somatic attunement include:

- Noticing where and how emotions manifest in your body.
- Tracking subtle shifts in physical sensations as emotions move.
- Using the body as a tuning fork to distinguish between authentic and conditioned responses.
- Following physical sensations to uncover emotions that may not be consciously recognized.

The body doesn't lie about emotional experience the way the thinking mind sometimes can. Learning to read its signals provides reliable guidance for reconnection.

> **"The body always leads us home ... if we can simply learn to trust sensation and stay with sensation long enough for it to reveal appropriate action." - Pat Ogden**

Emotional Archaeology: Uncovering Layers

Attunement often involves an archaeological process of gently uncovering layers of emotional experience. Beneath obvious or habitual emotions often lie deeper, more vulnerable feelings that hold important information.

This layering typically follows patterns like:

- Anger often covers hurt, fear, or grief.
- Numbness typically protects against overwhelming feelings.
- Anxiety frequently masks deeper fears about worthiness or safety.
- Chronic busyness may cover feelings of emptiness or purposelessness.

The process of uncovering these layers isn't about discarding the surface emotions but about expanding awareness to include what lies beneath them as well.

Attunement vs. Amplification: An Important Distinction

A crucial aspect of healthy attunement is distinguishing it from emotional amplification. Attunement involves bringing awareness to emotions as they authentically exist, while amplification artificially intensifies emotional reactions.

Signs of attunement:

- Emotions naturally rise and fall in awareness.
- Physical tension tends to release.
- Clarity emerges about the emotion's message.
- A sense of "rightness" or resonance appears.

Signs of unhelpful amplification:

- Emotions spiral in intensity without resolution.
- Physical tension increases.
- Rumination replaces insight.

- A sense of being stuck or overwhelmed predominates.

Developing the discernment to recognize the difference between attunement and amplification is an important skill in the alignment process.

PRACTICES FOR DEVELOPING ATTUNEMENT

Several approaches can strengthen your capacity for emotional attunement:

- **Focused breathing** — Using breath awareness to center attention in the body where emotions are felt
- **Gentle inquiry** — Asking questions like "What is this feeling trying to tell me?" or "What does this need?"
- **Expressive practices** — Using movement, sound, art, or writing to give form to emotions
- **Pendulation** — Moving attention between emotional activation and resource states to prevent overwhelm
- **Mindful naming** — Precisely labeling emotions with nuanced vocabulary that distinguishes subtle differences

These practices gradually restore your connection to the guidance system of your authentic emotions, allowing their wisdom to inform your choices and expressions.

Alright, let's get you dialed into your emotions, like tuning a radio to the right frequency. It's about listening to that inner wisdom, and here's how we do it:

First, let's start with focused breathing. It's not just about calming down, it's about getting grounded in your body, where your emotions live. Feel the breath, notice the sensations. Then, gentle inquiry – ask those questions, like "What's this feeling trying to tell me?" or "What do I need right now?" It's about having a conversation with your feelings, not ignoring them. And don't be afraid to express! Move your body, make some sounds, draw, write – whatever helps you give form to what you're feeling. It's about letting it out, not keeping it bottled up. Pendulation is key too. When things get intense, don't stay there. Move your attention back to something calming, something that feels good, then back to the feeling. It's about finding that balance.

And get specific with your words! Instead of just "sad," try "melancholy" or "grief." The more precise you are, the better you understand. It's like learning a new language, the language of your emotions. These practices, they're like little tools in your emotional toolkit. You use them bit by bit, and slowly, you start to hear that inner voice more clearly. You start to trust your gut, to know what you need. And that's where the change happens – when your choices and expressions come from that place of authentic emotional wisdom. You're not just reacting, you're responding, and that's a powerful way to live.

Stage 4: Aligned Action - Living from Integration

The final stage of the alignment process involves bringing your newfound emotional awareness into lived expression—translating internal reconnection into external change. This is where insight becomes embodied in new patterns of behavior and relationship.

Translating Awareness into Behavior

Aligned action bridges the gap between knowing and doing—between recognizing your authentic emotions and actually living from them. This translation involves:

- Expressing emotions in ways that honor both their authenticity and the context.
- Making choices guided by your emotional wisdom rather than conditioned patterns.
- Communicating your truth while maintaining connection.
- Creating external circumstances that support rather than undermine your authentic self.

This stage doesn't require dramatic life overhauls (though sometimes those do occur). More often, it involves subtle but significant shifts in how you express yourself and navigate your world.

Micro-Alignments: Small Acts with Big Impact

Alignment often begins with small moments of congruence that gradually expand into larger patterns. These micro-alignments might include:

- Pausing before automatically saying yes to a request.
- Naming a feeling in the moment it arises rather than afterward.
- Making a small choice based on what truly feels right rather than what you "should" do.
- Expressing a preference or need you would typically keep to yourself.
- Setting a minor boundary that honors your authentic limits.

These small acts might seem insignificant in isolation, but they create new neural pathways that make subsequent alignment easier. Each micro-alignment weakens conditioned patterns while strengthening authentic expression.

> **"It's the little details that are vital. Little things make big things happen." - John Wooden.**

Recovery from Misalignment: The Return Journey

Even with significant progress, you'll inevitably experience moments of returning to misalignment. These aren't failures but opportunities to practice the skill of recovery—the capacity to notice when you've disconnected and find your way back to authenticity.

Effective recovery involves:

- Recognizing misalignment without judgment or shame.
- Gently returning to awareness of your authentic experience.
- Accepting that the misalignment occurred for understandable reasons.
- Taking appropriate repair actions if others were affected.
- Learning from the experience rather than criticizing yourself for it.

This recovery capacity is perhaps more important than avoiding misalignment altogether, as it builds resilience and prevents temporary disconnections from becoming prolonged departures from authenticity.

Building Momentum: The Positive Cycle

As aligned actions accumulate, they create a positive feedback loop that reinforces continued growth. This momentum builds as:

- You experience the benefits of alignment firsthand.
- Your nervous system recognizes authenticity as increasingly safe.
- Others adjust to and often welcome your more authentic expression.
- Your confidence in navigating emotional territory grows.
- External circumstances gradually reorganize to support your authentic self.

This positive cycle doesn't eliminate challenges but creates a self-reinforcing trajectory toward greater alignment over time.

> **"Small deeds done are better than great deeds planned." - Peter Marshall.**

Imagine this: as you step into your authentic self, you'll feel it – a sense of safety settling into your nervous system. People around you, surprisingly, often respond positively to the real you, and with each step, your confidence blossoms. Suddenly, the world around you seems to shift, almost as if it's rearranging itself to support the person you were always meant to be. It's not just a theory; it's a lived experience, where your inner alignment creates a ripple effect in your outer world.

Practices for Aligned Action

Several approaches can support the translation of awareness into aligned living:

- **Values clarification** — Identifying your core values to guide decision-making
- **Authentic communication templates** — Learning phrases that express emotions clearly and responsibly.
- **Boundary setting practice** — Starting with smaller, less charged situations to build boundary-setting skills.
- **Accountability partnerships** — Sharing your alignment intentions with supportive others.
- **Environmental adjustments** — Making changes to your physical and social environment to support authenticity.

These practices create bridges between your internal work and external reality, allowing inner changes to manifest in tangible ways.

The Cyclical Nature of the Alignment Process

While I've presented these four stages sequentially, in practice the alignment process is cyclical rather than linear. You'll continually cycle through awareness, acceptance, attunement, and aligned action as you work with different emotional patterns and life circumstances.

Again, think of emotional alignment not as a destination, but as a dance, a continuous cycle of discovery and adjustment. You won't just "arrive" and stay there; life throws curveballs, old patterns resurface, and growth demands we evolve. It's a rhythm of self-awareness, compassion, and action, where you learn to recognize when you've drifted, gently course-correct, and embrace the ever-changing landscape of your inner world. This cycle, with its ebb and flow, is where true resilience is built, where you learn to trust your capacity to navigate the inevitable ups and downs, knowing that each return to alignment deepens your connection to your authentic self.

The capacity to navigate this cycle consciously—to recognize where you are in the process and what might support your next step—becomes a meta-skill that serves you in every area of emotional development.

> **"Life is a series of natural and spontaneous changes. Don't resist them; that only creates sorrow. Let reality be reality. Let things flow naturally forward in whatever way they like." - Lao Tzu.**

Creating a Safe Space for Emotional Exploration

The Foundation for Transformative Work

The alignment process we've explored requires a fundamental ingredient that's often overlooked: safety. Without sufficient safety—both internal and external—your system will naturally resist the vulnerability required for authentic emotional exploration. This resistance isn't a character flaw but an intelligent protection mechanism.

Creating conditions of safety doesn't happen by accident. It requires deliberate attention to both your inner landscape and your external environment. Let's explore how to establish the secure container that makes transformative emotional work possible.

Internal Safety: The Foundation for Exploration

Before considering external factors, the most essential form of safety is the one you create within yourself—the quality of relationship you maintain with your own experience. This internal safety determines whether emotions can emerge authentically or must remain hidden even from your own awareness.

Self-Compassion: The Essential Ingredient

At the heart of internal safety lies self-compassion—the practice of meeting your emotional experience with kindness rather than criticism. This compassionate stance creates the psychological safety needed for authentic emotions to surface.

Key elements of self-compassion include:

- **Mindfulness** — Clearly seeing your experience without avoidance or overidentification.
- **Common humanity** — Recognizing that struggles and difficult emotions are part of shared human experience.
- **Kindness** — Actively offering yourself warmth and understanding during challenging moments.

Research consistently shows that self-compassion—far from being self-indulgent—actually supports greater emotional resilience, healthier relationships, and more effective action than self-criticism. It creates the secure base from which authentic exploration becomes possible.

Practices to cultivate self-compassion include:

- Speaking to yourself as you would to a good friend facing similar challenges.
- Placing a hand on your heart during difficult moments to convey physical kindness.
- Using phrases like "This is a moment of suffering" to normalize your experience.
- Remembering that thousands of others are feeling similar emotions right now.

These simple practices dramatically change your relationship with emotional difficulty, creating an internal environment where authenticity can flourish.

Working with the Inner Critic: Transforming the Relationship

For many people, the greatest barrier to internal safety is a harsh inner critic—the internalized voice of judgment that comments on and evaluates your emotional responses. This critical voice often maintains the very patterns of misalignment you're working to transform.

Signs your inner critic is active include:

- Thoughts beginning with "I should" or "I shouldn't".
- Comparing yourself unfavorably to others.
- Using absolutist terms like "always" or "never".
- Making character assessments rather than observing behaviors.

Transforming your relationship with this inner critic involves not fighting against it but understanding its protective function. The critic typically develops as an internalized version of external criticism, trying to keep you safe by policing your behavior before others can reject you.

Approaches for working skillfully with the inner critic include:

- **Naming the critic** — Recognizing critical thoughts as coming from a part of you rather than defining you
- **Uncovering the fear** — Asking what the critic is afraid would happen if it stopped criticizing
- **Setting boundaries** — Firmly but compassionately limiting the critic's domain
- **Finding the kernel of care** — Identifying the positive intent beneath the criticism

This transformed relationship doesn't eliminate the inner critic but changes its role from harsh judge to constructive advisor, creating space for authentic emotions to emerge without immediate judgment.

Emotional Containment: Healthy Boundaries for Inner Work

Another aspect of internal safety involves developing what therapists call "containment"—the capacity to experience emotions fully without being overwhelmed by them. This containment creates boundaries around emotional experience that make exploration safe.

Signs of healthy emotional containment include:

- Being able to feel strong emotions without losing your sense of self.
- Maintaining perspective even while experiencing intensity.
- Recognizing that emotions are events in your experience, not your entire identity.

- Having access to internal resources during emotional challenges.

Containment doesn't mean suppressing or reducing emotions but rather developing the capacity to hold them within a strong enough vessel that they can be fully experienced without overwhelming your system.

Practices for developing emotional containment include:

- **Grounding techniques** — Physical practices that anchor you in the present moment.
- **Resource identification** — Recognizing and actively connecting to sources of internal strength.
- **Dual awareness** — Maintaining awareness of both the emotion and the larger context.
- **Temporal framing** — Remembering that all emotional states are temporary.

These containment practices create the secure boundaries within which authentic emotions can safely emerge and be explored.

Measure Principles: Approaching Difficult Emotions Gradually

A final aspect of internal safety involves the principle of measurement—approaching challenging emotional territory in manageable doses rather than all at once. This gradual approach prevents overwhelm while still allowing authentic reconnection.

Effective measure involves:

- Starting with less intense emotions before exploring more challenging ones.
- Taking breaks when activation becomes too high.
- Pendulating between difficult emotions and resource states.
- Honoring your current capacity rather than forcing greater exposure.

This measured approach isn't avoidance but wise pacing that respects your nervous system's need for integration time between periods of emotional activation.

Practices for effective measurement include:

- **The 10% principle** — Working with just a small percentage of an emotion's intensity.
- **Bookending** — Surrounding difficult emotional work with resource states before and after.
- **Micro-doses** — Brief exposure to challenging emotions with immediate return to safety.
- **The edge approach** — Finding the boundary where growth occurs without overwhelm.

These measurement practices allow you to gradually expand your capacity for emotional authenticity without the setbacks that come from overwhelm and retraumatization.

External Safety: Creating Supportive Environments

Beyond internal factors, the external environment significantly impacts your ability to engage in authentic emotional exploration. Creating contexts that support rather than undermine your alignment process is an essential aspect of this work.

Physical Space Considerations: The Container Matters

Your physical environment can either support or hinder emotional authenticity. Creating spaces that feel secure and comfortable provides an important foundation for inner work.

Elements that contribute to physically safe spaces include:

- Privacy for emotional expression without unwanted observation.
- Comfort that allows your body to relax rather than remain on guard.
- Personal touches that reflect and affirm your authentic identity.
- Natural elements that support groundedness and perspective.
- Minimal distractions that might pull you away from inner awareness

These environmental factors might seem secondary to the psychological aspects of safety, but your nervous system constantly scans your surroundings for cues of safety or danger, making physical space an important consideration.

> "You are a product of your environment. So choose the environment that will best develop you toward your objective." - W. Clement Stone.

Practices for creating supportive physical environments include:

- Designating a specific area in your home for emotional reflection.
- Using sensory elements (comfortable seating, pleasant scents, appropriate lighting) to signal safety.
- Removing or silencing digital devices that create distraction.
- Creating visual anchors that remind you of your values and resources.
- Ensuring basic needs like warmth, comfort, and privacy are met.

These environmental adjustments create a physical container that supports your psychological work.

Relationship Boundaries: Managing Who, When, and How You Share

Relationship boundaries are equally important for creating safety in your emotional alignment process. Not every relationship will support your authenticity equally, and discernment about where, when, and how you share is an essential skill.

Healthy relationship boundaries involve:

- Recognizing which relationships currently support authentic expression.
- Being selective about what aspects of your inner work you share and with whom.
- Communicating your needs clearly to those in your inner circle.
- Limiting exposure to relationships that actively undermine your authenticity.

This boundary-setting isn't about cutting people off but about making conscious choices about engagement based on the current reality of your relationships rather than idealized expectations.

Practices for establishing healthy relationship boundaries include:

- Creating a relationship map that identifies different levels of sharing.
- Preparing simple responses for situations where full authenticity isn't yet possible.
- Starting with "low-stakes" authentic expression in safer relationships.
- Finding at least one relationship where more complete authenticity is welcome.
- Setting clear time boundaries around potentially difficult interactions.

These boundaries protect your alignment process while still allowing for genuine connection appropriate to each relationship's current capacity.

> **"Daring to set boundaries is about having the courage to love ourselves, even when we risk disappointing others." - Brené Brown.**

COMMUNITY ASPECTS: FINDING YOUR AUTHENTICITY TRIBE

Beyond individual relationships, many people benefit from finding or creating communities that explicitly value and support emotional authenticity. These communities provide both modeling and reinforcement for your alignment journey.

Supportive communities might include:

- Formal groups focused on emotional growth or authentic living.

- Informal circles of friends committed to genuine connection.
- Online communities centered around emotional intelligence.
- Professional groups that value authentic leadership and communication.
- Spiritual or philosophical communities that emphasize integration and wholeness.

These communities create a counter-environment to broader cultural messages that often devalue emotional authenticity, providing validation that your journey matters and is shared by others.

Approaches for finding or creating supportive community include:

- Identifying existing groups aligned with authentic living values.
- Starting small with just one or two others interested in similar exploration.
- Looking for environments where vulnerability is met with respect rather than exploitation.
- Creating structured sharing spaces with clear agreements about interaction.
- Balancing challenge and support in the communities you choose.

These community connections provide external reinforcement for the internal changes you're making, creating social contexts where authenticity is valued rather than discouraged.

PROFESSIONAL SUPPORT: WHEN AND HOW TO SEEK ADDITIONAL GUIDANCE

For many people, professional support plays an important role in creating safety for deeper emotional work. Trained guides can help navigate challenging territory that might be difficult to traverse alone.

Professional support might include:

- Therapy with practitioners skilled in emotional work.
- Coaching focused on authenticity and alignment.
- Bodywork that addresses the physical aspects of emotional patterns.
- Group programs led by experienced facilitators.
- Spiritual direction that integrates emotional and existential dimensions.

These resources aren't necessary for everyone, but they can provide valuable containment and guidance, especially when working with deeply entrenched patterns or traumatic material.

Considerations when seeking professional support include:

- Finding practitioners whose approach resonates with your needs and values.
- Ensuring appropriate credentials and experience for the work you're undertaking.
- Trusting your sense of safety and rapport in the professional relationship.

- Being clear about your goals and boundaries in the work.
- Viewing professional support as complementary to your own inner resources.

Professional guidance works best when viewed not as a replacement for your own wisdom but as a supportive container that helps you access that wisdom more fully.

> **"No one is self-made; we are made up of thousands of others. Everyone who has ever done a kind deed for us, or spoken one word of encouragement to us, has entered into the makeup of our character and our thoughts, as well as our success." - George Matthew Adams.**

The Window of Tolerance: Staying Within Workable Ranges

A crucial concept for creating safety in emotional work is the "window of tolerance"—the zone where your nervous system can effectively process experience without moving into either hyperarousal (overwhelm) or hypoarousal (shutdown). Working within this window makes authentic exploration both possible and productive.

Recognizing Your Capacity: Emotional Bandwidth Awareness

Your window of tolerance is unique and dynamic, changing based on life circumstances, physical wellbeing, and emotional history. Developing awareness of your current capacity is an essential safety skill.

Signs you're within your window of tolerance include:

- Ability to think clearly while feeling emotions
- Curiosity about your experience rather than avoidance or fixation
- Physical signs of regulated nervous system (steady breathing, relaxed muscles)
- Emotional responsiveness without overwhelming reactivity
- Capacity to maintain connection with others while processing your own experience

This zone represents your optimal learning and integration state—where authentic emotions can be experienced without triggering protective disconnection.

Signs of Hyperarousal: Recognizing When You're Moving Beyond Your Edge

When you exceed the upper boundary of your window of tolerance, your system enters hyperarousal—a state of excessive activation that makes productive emotional work difficult.

Signs of hyperarousal include:

- Racing thoughts or obsessive focusing.
- Physical agitation or restlessness.
- Feeling emotionally flooded or overwhelmed.
- Difficulty concentrating or organizing thoughts.
- Impulse to fight or flee from the situation.

These signs indicate your nervous system has moved into a defensive state where survival concerns override the capacity for integration and learning.

Signs of Hypoarousal: Identifying Shutdown and Disconnection

Conversely, when you drop below the lower boundary of your window of tolerance, your system enters hypoarousal—a state of disconnection and shutdown that equally impedes authentic emotional work.

Signs of hypoarousal include:

- Emotional numbness or emptiness.
- Physical heaviness or fatigue.
- Difficulty accessing thoughts or feelings.
- Sense of disconnection or distance from experience.
- Impulse to freeze or dissociate.

These signs indicate your nervous system has moved into a protective shutdown where connection to experience is temporarily suspended.

Expanding Your Window: How to Gradually Increase Capacity

While respecting your current window of tolerance is important, you can gradually expand this window over time, increasing your capacity for emotional processing without overwhelm or shutdown.

Approaches for expanding your window include:

- Regular practices that build nervous system regulation.
- Gradually titrating exposure to challenging emotional material.
- Developing stronger internal and external resources.

- Working at the edges of your window without pushing far beyond them.
- Allowing sufficient integration time between periods of expansion.

This expansion doesn't happen through force or willpower but through consistent, gentle engagement with the edges of your current capacity.

PRACTICES FOR MAINTAINING REGULATION: TOOLS FOR STAYING WITHIN WORKABLE RANGES

Several practices can help you maintain or return to your window of tolerance during emotional exploration:

- **Orienting** — Shifting attention to your surroundings through sight, sound, or touch.
- **Bilateral stimulation** — Rhythmic left-right movement or tapping to regulate the nervous system.
- **Conscious breathing** — Using breath patterns that signal safety to your autonomic nervous system.
- **Physical movement** — Gentle activity that releases tension and resets activation levels.
- **Resource connection** — Actively bringing to mind images, memories, or relationships that create safety.

Let's keep you steady, even when things get intense. Think of these tools as your emotional anchors: grounding yourself with your senses, tapping into that calming rhythm, breathing like you're safe, moving to shake off tension, or picturing what brings you peace. They're not about running from feelings, but about staying grounded while you explore them. You're building your inner stability, so you can dive deep, learn, and grow, without getting overwhelmed. You've got this. These regulation tools aren't ways of avoiding emotions but rather methods for processing them within a range where integration can occur, making your emotional work both safer and more effective.

NAVIGATING EMOTIONAL INTENSITY: WHEN FEELINGS RUN STRONG

Even with all these safety measures in place, you'll inevitably encounter moments of intense emotion during your alignment journey. Having specific approaches for these high-intensity situations creates confidence that you can navigate whatever arises.

WORKING WITH EMOTIONAL TRIGGERS: APPROACHES FOR ACTIVATION

When specific triggers activate intense emotional responses, several approaches can help you maintain enough safety to work productively with the experience:

- **Recognition** — Simply naming that you've been triggered creates valuable space.
- **Time-shifting** — Reminding yourself that the triggering situation is happening now, not in the past.
- **Resource connection** — Actively bringing attention to sources of support and strength.
- **One emotion at a time** — Working with just a small percentage of the activated emotion.
- **Dual attention** — Maintaining awareness of both the trigger response and your present reality.

These approaches don't suppress the triggered response but create enough containment that you can work with it rather than being overwhelmed by it.

Grounding Techniques: Maintaining Connection to the Present

Grounding practices anchor you in present reality when intense emotions threaten to pull you into past patterns or future anxieties. These techniques create a stable foundation for authentic emotional processing.

Effective grounding techniques include:

- **Sensory awareness** — Noticing specific sensory details in your environment.
- **Physical contact** — Feeling the support of the floor, furniture, or earth beneath you.
- **Orientation in time and place** — Explicitly naming where and when you are.
- **Rhythmic movement** — Simple, repetitive physical actions that create predictability.
- **Present-focused language** — Using present-tense verbs when describing your experience.

These grounding practices maintain connection to the here-and-now, preventing the disorientation that can accompany intense emotional activation.

> **"Realize deeply that the present moment is all you ever have. Make the Now the primary focus of your life." - Eckhart Tolle.**

Pendulation: Moving Between Activation and Resource

When working with particularly challenging emotional material, the practice of pendulation—rhythmically moving attention between activation and resource states—creates safety by ensuring you don't remain too long in overwhelming territory.

Effective pendulation involves:

- Briefly touching into challenging emotional material.
- Intentionally shifting attention to a resource state or neutral focus.
- Allowing integration of the experience before returning to the activation.
- Noticing any shifts that occur between pendulation cycles.

- Respecting your current capacity for exposure duration.

This rhythmic movement between activation and resource mimics the natural oscillation of a healthy nervous system, creating dynamic stability rather than rigid control or chaotic overwhelm.

Integration Practices: Bringing Meaning to Intense Experiences

After periods of intense emotional work, integration practices help your system assimilate the experience, preventing fragmentation and supporting coherent growth.

Useful integration practices include:

- **Reflective writing** — Capturing insights and experiences without reactivating intensity
- **Gentle movement** — Walking, stretching, or other activities that support physical integration
- **Creative expression** — Using art, music, or other non-verbal methods to process experience
- **Structured meaning-making** — Identifying how the experience connects to your larger journey
- **Rest and restoration** — Allowing sufficient downtime for unconscious integration processes

These integration practices transform intense emotional experiences from potentially overwhelming events into meaningful components of your growth and healing. Journaling can be great to capture your emotions. Music can quickly alter and change our moods. Another key is to get proper rest. Make sure to recharge your battery.

EMERGENCY INTERVENTIONS: WHAT TO DO WHEN EMOTIONS FEEL OVERWHELMING

Despite all preparations, there may be moments when emotions temporarily exceed your capacity for processing. Having emergency interventions ready for these situations creates an essential safety net.

Effective emergency interventions include:

- **The 5-4-3-2-1 technique** — Sequentially noticing 5 things you see, 4 things you hear, 3 things you feel, 2 things you smell, and 1 thing you taste
- **Cold temperature exposure** — Holding ice, splashing cold water on your face, or stepping outside in cool air
- **Strong sensory input** — Using intense taste, smell, or touch to redirect attention
- **Physical discharge** — Pushing against a wall, squeezing a stress ball, or other safe physical release
- **Emergency contacts** — Reaching out to prepared support people when needed

These interventions aren't failures of your process but intelligent responses to temporary overwhelm, creating breathing room until you can return to more measured exploration.

The Ongoing Practice of Safety Creation

Creating safe space for emotional exploration isn't a one-time achievement but an ongoing practice that evolves with your changing needs and circumstances. What constitutes sufficient safety may shift dramatically as you develop greater capacity and encounter different life challenges.

The safety needed for emotional expression and authenticity isn't a one-and-done deal; it's an ongoing, living practice. Think of it like tending a garden – you don't just plant it and walk away. You're constantly weeding, watering, and ensuring the soil is fertile for growth. This means consistently checking in with yourself, noticing when your nervous system feels threatened, and actively choosing practices that bring you back to a place of groundedness. It's about building a consistent inner environment where vulnerability feels less like a risk and more like a natural part of being. You're learning to become your own safe harbor, your own trusted companion, creating a space where emotions can flow freely without judgment or fear. This ongoing work, this commitment to self-nurturing, is what allows authenticity to blossom and roots you in a deep sense of self-trust.

As we move into the next chapter on specific practices for emotional authenticity, remember that all the techniques we'll explore are most effective when practiced within the container of safety you've created. Each time you successfully navigate emotional territory while maintaining connection to yourself, you expand your capacity for authentic living in all areas of your life.

Chapter 4: Practices for Emotional Authenticity

Mindfulness Techniques for Emotional Awareness

Understanding the difference between your authentic and conditioned selves is powerful. Recognizing the alignment process is enlightening. But without practical skills to embody these insights, they remain interesting concepts rather than lived experience.

This is where many transformation journeys stall—in the gap between knowing and doing, between intellectual understanding and embodied practice. You might clearly see the patterns that disconnect you from your authentic self, but still find yourself caught in their familiar grip when emotions run high or relationships get challenging.

Chapter 4 is your practical field guide—the concrete skills and approaches that transform insight into action. Here we move from recognizing the path to actually walking it, from understanding authenticity to practicing it in real-world situations.

You'll discover mindfulness techniques that build the foundational awareness essential for authentic living. You'll learn communication strategies that allow you to express your truth while maintaining connection. You'll develop boundary-setting skills that protect your authentic self without creating unnecessary walls. And you'll explore the vulnerable territory where genuine connection becomes possible.

The beauty of practice is that it meets you exactly where you are. Whether emotional authenticity feels like completely foreign territory or somewhat familiar ground, these approaches offer next steps tailored to your unique journey. They build upon each other, creating tools you can draw from as different situations require different aspects of authentic expression. The skills in this chapter honor both dimensions, supporting your individual authenticity while enhancing your capacity for genuine connection.

The Gateway to Emotional Authenticity

At the foundation of all emotional authenticity lies a fundamental skill: the ability to be aware of your emotions as they unfold in real time. Without this awareness, even the most sophisticated emotional tools remain inaccessible, like instruments waiting to be played by hands that can't yet feel them.

Mindfulness—the practice of bringing non-judgmental awareness to your present-moment experience—provides the most direct path to developing this essential emotional awareness. Far from being an esoteric spiritual practice, mindfulness offers practical, evidence-based techniques for reconnecting with your authentic emotional landscape.

The Foundation of Mindful Awareness

When applied specifically to emotions, mindfulness involves bringing a particular quality of attention to your feeling states—observing them with curiosity rather than immediately reacting to or judging them. This creates a small but crucial space between emotional triggers and your responses, a space where choice becomes possible.

Three core components work together in mindful emotional awareness:

- **Attention:** Deliberately directing and sustaining your focus on current emotional experience.
- **Intention:** Consciously choosing to approach emotions with curiosity rather than avoidance.
- **Attitude:** Bringing qualities of kindness, patience, and non-judgment to whatever arises.

Many people misunderstand mindfulness as an attempt to empty the mind or achieve a state of perpetual calm. In reality, emotional mindfulness isn't about eliminating feelings or reaching some idealized state. Rather, it's about developing a different relationship with your emotions—one characterized by awareness, acceptance, and wise discernment rather than reactivity or suppression.

The neuroscience behind mindfulness reveals why this practice is so transformative for emotional intelligence. Regular mindfulness practice actually changes your brain in several important ways:

- Strengthening connections between your prefrontal cortex (executive function) and limbic system (emotional centers).
- Reducing activity in the default mode network associated with rumination and worry.
- Increasing gray matter density in areas responsible for self-awareness and compassion.
- Enhancing your nervous system's capacity to return to balance after emotional activation.

These neurological changes explain why mindfulness practitioners report not that they stop having emotions, but that they develop a more spacious, less reactive relationship with their emotional experiences. As one client described it: "I still feel everything—sometimes even more intensely—but I'm no longer hijacked by my feelings. There's room to breathe around them."

Formal Mindfulness Practices for Emotional Intelligence

While mindfulness can eventually become an integrated aspect of daily life, formal practices provide the training ground where this skill develops. Think of these structured practices as deliberate workouts for your attention muscle, gradually building the capacity that will serve you in real-world emotional situations.

Here are several formal practices specifically adapted for emotional awareness:

Three-Minute Breathing Space

This brief practice offers a powerful reset for your emotional awareness, making it ideal for busy schedules or moments when you notice emotional activation beginning.

1. **Awareness (1 minute):** Begin by bringing awareness to your current experience, noting thoughts, feelings, and bodily sensations without trying to change them. Simply ask: "What's happening for me right now?"
2. **Gathering Attention (1 minute):** Gently narrow your focus to the physical sensations of breathing, using each breath as an anchor for your attention. When the mind wanders (which it will), simply notice this and return to the breath.

3. **Expanding Awareness (1 minute):** Broaden your attention to include your whole body, particularly noticing any areas holding emotional tension. Hold your full experience in this expanded awareness.

This practice can serve as an emotional check-in throughout your day, helping you catch emotional patterns earlier and creating space for more conscious responses.

Emotional Body Scan

Your body constantly communicates emotional information through physical sensations, but much of this data goes unnoticed. The emotional body scan helps you access this wisdom by systematically bringing awareness to bodily sensations associated with feelings.

> **"If you listen to your body when it whispers, you won't have to hear it scream."**
> **- Unknown.**

1. Find a comfortable position sitting or lying down where you can remain alert but relaxed.
2. Begin with several deep breaths, allowing your attention to settle into your body.
3. Starting at either your head or feet, slowly move your attention through each part of your body, noticing any sensations present without trying to change them.
4. When you encounter areas of tension, heaviness, or other strong sensations, pause and explore with curiosity: "What emotion might be expressing itself through this physical feeling?"
5. Continue until you've scanned your entire body, noting connections between physical sensations and emotional states.

This practice bypasses the analytical mind to access emotional information directly through the body, often revealing feelings that weren't previously in your awareness.

RAIN Practice for Difficult Emotions

Developed by meditation teacher Tara Brach, the RAIN practice offers a structured approach for working mindfully with challenging emotions. The acronym stands for:

R - Recognize: Simply note the emotion that's present: "Ah, this is anxiety," or "I'm feeling shame right now." This recognition interrupts automatic reactivity.

A - Allow: Permit the emotion to be present without immediately trying to fix, change, or escape it. This might involve silently saying, "Let me just be with this for now" or "I consent to feel this."

I - Investigate: Bring curious attention to how this emotion manifests in your body, what thoughts accompany it, and what it might be trying to tell you. This investigation happens with kindness, not analytical problem-solving.

N - Nurture: Offer compassion to yourself in the midst of this feeling. Ask, "What does this part of me need right now?" and respond with kindness, perhaps through gentle words, a self-compassionate gesture, or simply a quality of tender attention.

The RAIN practice transforms your relationship with difficult emotions from adversarial to compassionate, creating the conditions for authentic expression rather than reactive suppression or amplification.

> **"Success is a journey, not a destination. The doing is often more important than the outcome." - Arthur Ashe.**

MINDFUL JOURNALING

Writing can powerfully enhance emotional awareness when approached mindfully. Unlike regular journaling, mindful journaling emphasizes present-moment awareness over analysis or problem-solving.

Try this approach:

1. Set aside 5-15 minutes in a quiet space with minimal distractions.
2. Begin by taking a few mindful breaths to center your attention in the present.
3. Ask yourself, "What am I feeling right now?" and begin writing without censoring or planning.
4. When you notice your mind shifting to analysis, judgment, or storytelling, gently bring your attention back to direct emotional experience.
5. Include notes about physical sensations and where you feel emotions in your body.
6. End by reading what you've written with compassionate awareness.

This practice develops not only emotional recognition but also the vocabulary to express nuanced feelings, an essential component of emotional authenticity.

SAFE PLACE VISUALIZATION

Creating an internal refuge of safety supports exploration of challenging emotions. This visualization practice establishes a mental space you can return to whenever emotional intensity feels overwhelming.

1. Find a comfortable position and take several grounding breaths.
2. Imagine a place—real or imagined—where you feel completely safe, accepted, and at peace.
3. Build this image with sensory detail: What do you see, hear, smell, and feel in this place?
4. Notice the sensations in your body as you imagine being in this safe place.

5. When the image feels vivid and stabilizing, mentally "bookmark" it as a resource.
6. Practice returning to this safe place briefly throughout your day.

This practice doesn't avoid difficult emotions but creates the secure base from which authentic emotional exploration becomes possible.

Informal Mindfulness in Daily Life

While formal practices build the foundation, informal mindfulness woven throughout your day creates lasting change in your relationship with emotions. These approaches integrate awareness into your existing activities rather than requiring additional time commitments.

Micro-Moments of Awareness

Brief check-ins throughout your day can dramatically increase emotional awareness with minimal disruption to your schedule. Try these micro-practices:

- **Traffic Light Moments:** Each time you stop at a red light, take three conscious breaths and notice how you're feeling.
- **Door Frame Practice:** Use walking through doorways as a trigger to briefly check in with your emotional state.
- **Notification Awareness:** When your phone chimes with a notification, pause to notice your emotional response before checking it.
- **Hand-Washing Check-In:** Use the time while washing your hands to scan your current emotional state.
- **Waiting Moments:** Transform waiting time (in lines, for appointments, etc.) into opportunities for emotional awareness.

These micro-moments prevent emotions from building up unnoticed throughout the day, allowing for earlier recognition and more skillful responses.

Mindful Transitions

Transitions between activities offer natural opportunities for emotional awareness. Instead of rushing from one task to another, use these transition points as mindful pauses:

1. As you complete one activity, take a moment to notice how it affected your emotional state.
2. Take three conscious breaths, feeling your feet on the ground.
3. Set a clear intention for how you want to approach the next activity.
4. Begin the new task with full presence.

This practice prevents emotional residue from one situation from unconsciously influencing the next, creating cleaner emotional boundaries between different parts of your day.

Environmental Reminders

Physical cues in your environment can prompt emotional awareness when attention naturally wanders. Try placing simple reminders in locations you encounter regularly:

- A small dot sticker on your computer monitor.
- A special item on your desk or in your pocket.
- A specific image as your phone background.
- A meaningful symbol worn as jewelry.
- A distinctive object in rooms you frequent.

When you notice these cues, use them as triggers to check in with your emotional state, creating dozens of awareness moments throughout your day.

"Emotion-Spotting" Practice

This practice involves deliberately noticing emotions—both your own and others'—as you move through your day. Like a birdwatcher looking for different species, become an observer of emotional states:

- Notice subtle facial expressions revealing feelings.
- Pay attention to shifts in your own emotional tone.
- Observe emotional climate in meetings or gatherings.
- Notice emotional content in media you consume.
- Identify emotional subtext in conversations.

This practice develops your emotional recognition skills while normalizing the constant presence of emotions in human experience.

Digital Mindfulness

Technology often pulls us away from emotional awareness, but with intention, it can become a support rather than a hindrance:

- Set regular "device-free" periods to check in with your emotional state.
- Use apps designed to prompt mindful awareness at intervals.
- Create boundaries around emotionally provocative content.
- Practice noticing your emotional state before and after social media use.
- Use digital sunset practices to support emotional regulation before sleep.

These practices transform your relationship with technology from a source of emotional distraction to a potential ally in awareness.

Developing Sustainable Practice

The most powerful mindfulness practice is the one you'll actually do consistently. Rather than aiming for an idealized version of practice, focus on making emotional awareness sustainable in your real life.

Starting Small

One of the biggest obstacles to developing mindfulness is the misconception that it requires large time commitments. In reality, consistency matters far more than duration, especially for emotional awareness.

Try these approaches:

- Begin with just one minute of formal practice daily.
- Choose a single daily activity for informal mindfulness.
- Use the "just three breaths" practice whenever you remember.
- Focus on quality of attention rather than quantity of time.
- Build gradually based on what feels sustainable.

This approach prevents the perfectionism that often derails practice before it can establish roots in your life.

Personalization

There is no one-size-fits-all approach to mindfulness. Experimenting to find what resonates with your particular temperament and circumstances creates a sustainable practice:

- If you're physically active, try movement-based mindfulness like walking meditation.
- If you're analytical, practices with more cognitive structure might appeal.
- If you're creative, visualization or artistic expression might be your gateway.
- If you're socially oriented, consider group practice or relational mindfulness.
- If you're busy, emphasize brief practices integrated into existing activities.

The best practice is one that fits naturally into your life and personality rather than requiring you to become someone you're not.

> **"Practice isn't the thing you do once you're good. It's the thing you do that makes you good."** - Malcolm Gladwell.

OVERCOMING COMMON OBSTACLES

Every mindfulness practitioner encounters challenges. Having strategies ready for common obstacles prevents them from derailing your progress:

For the wandering mind: Remember that noticing your mind has wandered IS the practice. Each time you notice and gently return your attention, you're strengthening your mindfulness muscle.

For restlessness: Try shorter practices or movement-based mindfulness when restlessness is strong. Sometimes walking meditation works better than sitting.

For sleepiness: Practice with eyes open, try a more upright posture, or schedule practice for times when you're naturally more alert.

For resistance: Start with just one minute, or focus on informal practices that don't require setting aside special time.

For forgetting: Use environmental cues, calendar reminders, or habit stacking (connecting practice to an existing habit) to support remembering.

These approaches transform obstacles from practice-ending roadblocks to opportunities for deepening your understanding.

TRACKING PROGRESS

Progress in mindfulness often happens subtly, with changes that are easy to miss without deliberate attention. Noticing these shifts reinforces your motivation:

- Increased moments of catching emotional reactions before acting on them.
- More nuanced recognition of emotional states ("I'm not just angry but also hurt").
- Quicker recovery from emotional activation.
- Greater willingness to experience difficult emotions without avoidance.
- More frequent moments of authentic expression.

Periodically reflecting on these changes—perhaps in a journal or conversation with a supportive person—helps sustain practice through challenging periods.

> **"Without continual growth and progress, such words as improvement, achievement, and success have no meaning." - Benjamin Franklin.**

Building Mindfulness into Existing Routines

Rather than viewing mindfulness as another task on your to-do list, look for ways to infuse awareness into activities you're already doing:

- Transform your morning coffee or tea into a mindfulness ritual.
- Practice awareness of emotional states during your commute.
- Bring mindful attention to the first and last moments of your workday.
- Use workout time as an opportunity for embodied awareness.
- Practice mindful listening during conversations you're already having.

This integration approach makes mindfulness a way of living rather than a separate activity competing for your limited time.

The Journey of Practice

Learning something new, whether it's a skill, a concept, or even a way of being, is just the first step. That initial spark of understanding is exciting, but it's the practice that truly transforms knowledge into wisdom. Practice is where the abstract becomes concrete, where the "I know" turns into "I can." It's where you stumble, adjust, and refine, turning raw information into an integrated part of your being.

And it's not just about repetition; it's about mindful engagement. It's about bringing intention and curiosity to each attempt, noticing the subtle nuances, the small shifts in understanding. It's about allowing yourself to be a beginner, to make mistakes, and to learn from them. Every time you practice, you're building new neural pathways, strengthening the connection between your mind and your actions. You're not just memorizing; you're embodying the knowledge, making it a part of your muscle memory, your emotional landscape, your very essence.

What matters most is not perfection but persistence—continuing to return your attention to emotional awareness even after inevitable periods of forgetting or distraction. Each time you notice an emotion as it arises, you strengthen the foundation for authentic living.

In the next section, we'll build on this awareness by exploring communication strategies that allow you to express your authentic emotions effectively, translating inner awareness into meaningful connection with others.

Bridging Inner Awareness and Outer Connection

Once you've developed greater awareness of your authentic emotions, the next challenge emerges: how do you express these feelings in ways that honor your truth while maintaining connection with others? This is where the art of authentic communication becomes essential.

Authentic communication isn't about unfiltered emotional expression or saying whatever comes to mind regardless of impact. Rather, it's about finding ways to express your emotional truth that are both honest and skillful—honoring your authenticity while respecting the complexity of human relationships.

The Elements of Authentic Communication

Authentic communication integrates several key elements that work together to create both truthfulness and connection. When any of these elements is missing, communication often fails to achieve either authenticity or meaningful engagement.

Congruence: Aligning Your Channels of Expression

Perhaps the most fundamental aspect of authentic communication is congruence—alignment between your words, tone of voice, facial expressions, and body language. This alignment is what others intuitively read as truthfulness, often without conscious awareness.

Incongruence happens when these channels send mixed messages:

- Saying "I'm fine" through clenched teeth.
- Smiling while expressing anger or hurt.
- Using caring words with a cold or dismissive tone.
- Nodding agreement while your body tenses in resistance.

This misalignment creates confusion for listeners and disconnection for you, as your authentic emotion leaks through despite verbal denials. Even when others can't name the specific incongruence, they sense something is "off" in the communication.

> **"Personal congruence consists in maintaining the coherence between what you experience at any given moment and what your senses express. That is true health." - Moshe Feldenkrais.**

Developing congruence involves:

- Noticing when your words and nonverbal signals don't match.

- Pausing to align your expression with your authentic feeling before speaking.
- Being willing to acknowledge confusion or mixed feelings rather than presenting false certainty.
- Practicing with smaller emotions before attempting congruence with more challenging feelings.

This alignment creates the foundation for communications that feel truthful both to you and your listeners.

Emotional Vocabulary: Finding Words for Feelings

Many of us were raised with extremely limited emotional vocabulary—perhaps just "good," "bad," "fine," and a handful of other vague terms. This limitation makes precise emotional communication nearly impossible, like trying to paint with only three colors.

Expanding your emotional vocabulary involves:

- Learning to distinguish between similar emotions (irritation vs. anger vs. rage).
- Recognizing mixed emotional states ("I feel both disappointed and relieved").
- Developing language for emotional nuance and intensity.
- Practicing naming emotions with increasing specificity.

This expanded vocabulary isn't about impressing others with sophisticated terminology but about giving yourself the tools to accurately translate internal experience into shared understanding.

Resources for building emotional vocabulary include:

- Emotion wheels that show relationships between feelings.
- Word lists organized by emotional families.
- Reading emotionally nuanced literature and poetry.
- Regular practice naming your own emotional states with precision.

As your vocabulary expands, you'll find yourself able to communicate feelings that previously remained vague and inaccessible both to yourself and others.

Timing: The When of Authentic Expression

Authentic communication isn't just about what you express but when you express it. Timing can significantly impact whether your truth creates connection or conflict.

Considerations for effective timing include:

- **Emotional readiness:** Sometimes you need time to process feelings before expressing them clearly.
- **Recipient readiness:** Considering whether others are in a state to hear your truth.
- **Contextual appropriateness:** Some settings support authentic exchange better than others.

- **Energy levels:** Communicating complex emotions requires resources from both speaker and listener.
- **Follow-up availability:** Ensuring there's time to address responses to your communication.

Skillful timing doesn't mean indefinitely postponing difficult communications. Rather, it means choosing moments that maximize the potential for genuine understanding and connection.

Context Awareness: Adapting Without Compromising

Authentic communication looks different across various contexts and relationships. The art is learning to adapt your expression to different environments without abandoning your core truth.

This adaptation involves:

- Recognizing the emotional culture of different contexts (family, workplace, social circles).
- Adjusting the form of your expression while maintaining its essence.
- Finding appropriate language for various settings.
- Being selective about depth and detail while remaining truthful.
- Respecting different relationship boundaries without becoming inauthentic.

This flexibility isn't about being fake in different contexts but about translating your truth into forms that can be received in various environments—like speaking the same message in different languages depending on who's listening.

> **"It is not the strongest of the species that survives, nor the most intelligent that survives. It is the one that is most adaptable to change." - Charles Darwin.**

The Balance of Honesty and Care: Truth with Heart

Perhaps the greatest misconception about authentic communication is that it requires choosing between complete honesty and caring for others. In reality, the most effective authentic communication integrates both.

This integration involves:

- Recognizing that how you deliver truth affects how it's received
- Distinguishing between honesty (sharing your truth) and unfiltered expression (dumping unprocessed emotions)
- Speaking from your experience rather than presenting judgments as facts
- Considering the purpose of your communication—connection vs. merely unburdening yourself
- Taking responsibility for your intention in sharing

When honesty and care work together, authentic communication becomes not a weapon that creates distance but a bridge that connects your truth with others' capacity to hear it.

> **"Tact is the knack of making a point without making an enemy." - Isaac Newton.**

Feeling Identification: Your Emotional Response

The second component involves clearly expressing your feelings that arose in response to the situation, without implying that others caused these feelings or are responsible for them.

Compare:

- **Blaming:** "You made me feel disrespected and insignificant."
- **Ownership:** "I felt frustrated and unheard when I was interrupted."

The first approach implicitly holds others responsible for your emotions, typically triggering defensiveness. The second owns your feeling response while still connecting it to the triggering situation.

Effective feeling identification involves:

- Using clear feeling words rather than thoughts disguised as feelings ("I feel that you...")
- Taking responsibility for your emotional responses
- Distinguishing between feelings and interpretations
- Being willing to share vulnerable primary emotions rather than just secondary reactions

This honest naming of feelings creates the emotional authenticity at the heart of this communication approach.

Needs Connection: What Matters to You

The third component connects your feelings to your underlying needs or values—the universal human requirements that generate emotional responses when met or unmet.

Compare:

- **Without needs:** "I felt hurt because you were late."
- **With needs:** "I felt hurt because I need reliability and respect for our agreements."

The first statement implicitly suggests the other person's behavior was wrong. The second reveals what's important to you, creating potential for understanding rather than argument about right and wrong.

Connecting to needs involves:

- Identifying the universal human needs behind your emotional reactions.
- Recognizing that all humans share the same basic needs.
- Distinguishing needs (universal) from strategies (specific ways to meet needs).
- Being willing to be vulnerable about what truly matters to you.

This needs connection transforms complaints into invitations for deeper understanding, revealing the legitimate care beneath difficult emotions.

Clear Requests: Moving Forward

The final component involves making specific, doable requests rather than demands—asking for actions that might help meet your needs in the current situation or similar future scenarios.

Effective requests:

- Are specific and concrete rather than vague.
- Ask for positive actions (what you want) rather than what you don't want.
- Remain open to hearing "no" or negotiating alternatives.
- Include the purpose behind the request when helpful.
- Consider what's actually doable for the other person.

This approach transforms potentially destructive emotional expression into constructive invitations for positive change, maintaining connection while honoring your authentic needs.

Receiving Others' Communication: The Other Side

Authentic communication isn't just about expression but also reception—developing the capacity to hear others' truth even when it's challenging. The same NVC framework provides guidance for receiving communication with openness:

- Listen for the observations (what happened from their perspective).
- Hear the feelings beneath their words, even when unclearly expressed.
- Connect to the needs or values that matter to them.
- Focus on requests that might address the situation.

This receptive capacity creates the space for others to express their authenticity, completing the circle of genuine communication.

Difficult Conversations with Authenticity

Difficult conversations, while often dreaded, are actually fertile ground for cultivating authenticity. When we avoid these challenging exchanges, we're often dodging vulnerability, suppressing our true feelings, and maintaining a facade of comfort. But authenticity thrives in honesty, even when it's uncomfortable. By choosing to speak our truth, to express our needs and boundaries, we're signaling to ourselves and others that we value genuine connection over superficial harmony. These conversations force us to confront our fears, clarify our values, and stand in our integrity. They're a crucible where we forge a stronger sense of self.

Furthermore, difficult conversations can dismantle the roles we unconsciously play in relationships. When we're trapped in conditioned patterns of people-pleasing or conflict avoidance, we sacrifice authenticity for the illusion of safety. By engaging in these conversations, we're breaking those patterns, showing up as our full selves, and inviting others to do the same. They can reveal hidden dynamics, clear up misunderstandings, and create space for deeper, more meaningful connections. While they might be uncomfortable in the moment, they pave the way for relationships built on honesty, respect, and genuine understanding, which are the cornerstones of authentic living.

> **"Difficult conversations do not just involve feelings, they are at their very core about feelings." - Douglas Stone, Bruce Patton, and Sheila Heen."**

Preparation Practices: Creating Inner Readiness

Preparation for challenging conversations isn't about scripting every word but about creating the internal conditions for authentic presence:

- **Emotional check-in:** Identifying and acknowledging your feelings before the conversation.
- **Needs clarification:** Getting clear about what truly matters to you in this situation.
- **Intention setting:** Deciding what you want to create through the conversation beyond just expressing yourself.
- **Centering practice:** Using breath, movement, or other techniques to ground yourself.
- **Compassion cultivation:** Generating goodwill toward yourself and the other person.

This preparation creates an internal foundation that supports authentic expression even when external circumstances become challenging.

Starting Points: Opening Lines That Set the Tone

How you begin difficult conversations significantly impacts their trajectory. Effective openings:

- Signal your desire for mutual understanding rather than battle.

- Acknowledge the potential discomfort or importance of the topic.
- Invite collaboration rather than presenting demands.
- Show your willingness to hear the other perspective.
- Set a realistic time frame appropriate to the topic.

Examples of effective openings include:

- "I'd like to talk about something that's been on my mind. Is this a good time, or would another time work better?"
- "I've noticed something in our interaction that feels uncomfortable for me. I'd like to understand it better together."
- "This is difficult for me to bring up, but I care enough about our relationship to have this conversation."

These openings create a container for authentic exchange that invites rather than demands engagement.

> **"Think twice before you speak, because your words and influence will plant the seed of either success or failure in the mind of another." - Napoleon Hill.**

NAVIGATING DEFENSIVE RESPONSES: MAINTAINING CONNECTION

Even with careful preparation and thoughtful openings, authentic communication sometimes triggers defensive responses. Having strategies to navigate these reactions helps maintain connection without abandoning your truth:

- **Reflective listening:** Pausing to ensure you understand their perspective before continuing.
- **Acknowledging impact:** Recognizing how your communication is affecting them.
- **Returning to common ground:** Reaffirming shared values or goals.
- **Offering choice:** Creating options for how to proceed rather than pushing ahead.
- **Suggesting breaks:** Recognizing when temporary pauses might be helpful.

These approaches demonstrate that your commitment to connection is as strong as your commitment to truth, making continued dialogue more likely.

RECOVERY FROM COMMUNICATION BREAKDOWNS: REPAIR STRATEGIES

Despite best efforts, authentic communication sometimes leads to misunderstandings or emotional reactions that derail connection. Having repair strategies ready helps transform these moments from communication failures into opportunities for deeper understanding:

- **Acknowledging the disconnect:** Simply naming that the conversation has gone off track.

- **Taking responsibility for your contribution:** Recognizing your part without over-apologizing.
- **Clarifying misunderstandings:** Restating your intention or meaning.
- **Suggesting a reset:** Offering to approach the topic differently.
- **Following up later:** Recognizing when time and space might be needed before reconnection.

These repair efforts demonstrate that authentic communication includes not just speaking your truth but maintaining your commitment to understanding even when challenges arise. As you become more aware of your triggers and emotions, you will also learn how to become more aware of other peoples triggers and emotions. This growth allows you to interact and to respond better.

One client described a powerful repair moment: "After our argument spiraled, I simply said, 'This isn't going how I hoped. I really want to understand your perspective, and I also want to feel understood. Could we try again?' Those few sentences completely shifted the energy."

Self-Compassion for Imperfect Conversations: Managing Expectations

Perhaps the most important support for authentic communication is maintaining realistic expectations and self-compassion when conversations don't go as planned:

- Recognizing that perfect communication doesn't exist.
- Acknowledging that skill development takes time and practice.
- Appreciating your courage in attempting authentic expression.
- Seeing challenging conversations as learning opportunities rather than failures.
- Extending the same understanding to yourself that you would offer to others

This self-compassion creates the emotional safety to continue practicing authentic communication despite inevitable imperfect attempts, allowing growth rather than discouragement from difficulties.

Digital Communication and Authenticity

In our world today, a significant portion of our communication happens through digital channels, creating both challenges and opportunities for authentic expression.

Emotional Expression in Text: Challenges and Strategies

Text-based communication removes many of the nonverbal cues that support emotional understanding, creating specific challenges for authentic expression:

- **Emotion misinterpretation:** Without tone and facial cues, feelings are easily misread.

- **Delayed feedback:** The gap between sending and response creates uncertainty.
- **Permanence concerns:** The record of written communication can inhibit authenticity.
- **Context collapse:** Different audiences may access the same communication.

Strategies for more authentic text communication include:

- Being more explicit about emotional content than you would in person.
- Using emojis, GIFs, or other tools to supplement emotional tone.
- Checking understanding more frequently than in face-to-face conversation.
- Considering voice or video alternatives for emotionally complex topics.
- Reading important messages aloud before sending to check how they might be received.

These approaches don't eliminate the limitations of text but create more room for emotional authenticity within them.

SOCIAL MEDIA AUTHENTICITY: NAVIGATING PERFORMATIVE PRESSURES

Social media platforms create unique challenges for authentic communication, often encouraging performative rather than genuine expression. Navigating these spaces authentically involves:

- Clarifying your purpose for engagement on each platform
- Setting intentional boundaries around what you choose to share and why
- Recognizing the difference between strategic vulnerability and true authenticity
- Being willing to engage more deeply in private channels when appropriate
- Regularly assessing whether your online presence reflects your values

This intentional approach allows social media to become a space for aspects of authentic expression rather than a pressure toward performative sharing.

VIDEO COMMUNICATION SKILLS: PRESENCE PRACTICES FOR VIRTUAL INTERACTION

Video calls have become ubiquitous, creating a hybrid communication environment with its own requirements for authentic presence. Skills for more authentic video communication include:

- Creating physical spaces that support your comfortable presence.
- Practicing looking at the camera to create the experience of eye contact.
- Being mindful of the additional cognitive load of video calls.
- Using chat features to supplement verbal communication when helpful.
- Acknowledging the limitations of the medium rather than pretending they don't exist.

These adjustments help translate in-person authenticity skills to digital environments that are increasingly central to our communication landscape.

Boundaries in Digital Spaces: Protecting Authentic Expression

Digital spaces often create implicit pressure for constant availability and immediate response, potentially undermining thoughtful authentic communication. Establishing clear boundaries helps protect your capacity for meaningful engagement:

- Setting clear expectations about response times.
- Creating technology-free spaces and times in your life.
- Being selective about notification settings.
- Practicing "slow communication" for important topics.
- Using asynchronous methods (voice memos, thoughtful emails) when real-time exchange isn't essential.

These boundaries don't diminish connection but rather create the conditions for more meaningful engagement when you do communicate.

Intentional Disconnection: The Role of Digital Breaks

Perhaps counterintuitively, regular periods of intentional disconnection from digital communication often enhance authentic expression when you do engage. These breaks allow:

- Reconnection with your direct experience without mediation.
- Recovery of attentional resources depleted by constant connectivity.
- Space for reflection on what's truly important to communicate.
- Reset of stimulation thresholds often elevated by digital engagement.
- Appreciation for the value of connection when you return.

Building regular digital disconnection into your rhythm—whether for hours, days, or longer periods—supports the internal awareness that makes authentic communication possible.

The Practice of Authentic Communication

Like any significant skill, authentic communication develops through practice rather than perfect implementation from the start. Begin with lower-stakes situations before applying these approaches to your most challenging relationships or topics.

Appropriate contexts for early practice include:

- Expressing positive emotions authentically (often easier than difficult feelings).
- Practicing with trusted friends who support your growth.
- Applying frameworks to written reflection before direct conversation.
- Using structured exercises with partners willing to explore together.
- Addressing minor irritations before major conflicts.

This graduated approach builds your capacity gradually, creating the foundation for authentic communication even in your most challenging relationships.

Honest communication can feel daunting. It requires vulnerability, courage, and a willingness to step outside your comfort zone. But remember, it's a skill, like any other, that develops with practice. Start small, with safe people and low-stakes situations. Focus on expressing your feelings without blame or judgment, using "I" statements to own your experience. As you become more comfortable, you'll find your voice growing stronger, your boundaries clearer, and your relationships more authentic.

And here's the beautiful truth: when you model honesty, you invite others to do the same, creating a chain reaction of authenticity that changes your relationships and your life. It's an act of self-empowerment, a declaration that you deserve to be seen and heard, and that your truth matters.

In the next section, we'll explore emotional boundaries—the essential limits that protect your authentic self while creating the safety needed for genuine connection.

Setting Emotional Boundaries

Authentic emotional expression doesn't mean sharing everything with everyone all the time. In fact, one of the most essential components of emotional authenticity is the ability to set and maintain healthy boundaries—the invisible lines that define where you end and others begin.

Emotional boundaries protect your authentic self while creating the safety necessary for genuine connection. Far from being barriers to intimacy, well-defined boundaries actually make deeper connections possible by establishing the respect and clarity required for trust to flourish.

Understanding Emotional Boundaries

Despite their importance, emotional boundaries remain widely misunderstood. Many people either view boundaries as selfish walls that keep others out or fail to establish them altogether, creating confusion and resentment in their relationships.

DEFINING HEALTHY BOUNDARIES: WHAT THEY ARE AND AREN'T

Healthy emotional boundaries are:

- Clear limits that define acceptable behavior toward you.
- Guidelines about how you want to be treated.
- Expressions of self-respect and personal values.
- Flexible frameworks that evolve with circumstances and relationships.
- Protective without being isolating.

They are not:

- Attempts to control others' behavior or emotions.
- Rigid walls that prevent authentic connection.
- Punishments or weapons in relationship conflicts.
- One-size-fits-all rules that apply identically in all contexts.
- Excuses to avoid vulnerability or emotional intimacy.

Understanding these distinctions helps clarify that boundaries are not about rejection or distance but about creating the conditions where authentic connection can safely flourish.

THE CONNECTION TO AUTHENTICITY: HOW BOUNDARIES PROTECT YOUR TRUE SELF

Boundaries and authenticity share an essential relationship—you cannot fully express your authentic self without the protection boundaries provide. Here's why:

- Boundaries prevent your emotional energy from being drained by inappropriate demands.
- They create space for you to hear your own internal voice amidst external pressures.
- They protect you from taking on others' emotions as if they were your own.
- They allow you to stay connected to your values even in challenging situations.
- They differentiate between compassion (feeling with others) and emotional absorption.

Without these protective boundaries, your authentic self becomes vulnerable to being overwhelmed, manipulated, or lost entirely in others' expectations and emotional states.

Building these boundaries isn't always easy. It requires clarity, courage, and sometimes, uncomfortable conversations. However, the rewards are immense. When you protect your boundaries, you create space for your true self to flourish. You'll find yourself less resentful, more energized, and more capable of showing up authentically in your relationships. You'll discover that saying "no" to what drains you allows you to say "yes" to what truly nourishes you. And here's the empowering truth: healthy boundaries actually enhance connection. When people know where your limits are, they can interact with you more respectfully and genuinely, fostering trust and deeper intimacy. You're not pushing people away; you're inviting them to meet you on your terms, in a space where authenticity thrives.

As one client eloquently put it: "Before I learned about boundaries, I was like a house without doors—anyone could walk in and rearrange my emotional furniture. Now I decide who gets to come in and what they can touch."

> **"Boundaries are a part of self-care. They are healthy, normal, and necessary." - Doreen Virtue.**

COMMON BOUNDARY CONFUSION: WALLS, DEMANDS, AND TRUE BOUNDARIES

Many boundary difficulties stem from confusion about what constitutes a genuine boundary versus other types of interpersonal behavior:

Boundaries vs. Walls

- Boundaries allow selective connection; walls prevent all connection.
- Boundaries are permeable and context-sensitive; walls are rigid and absolute.
- Boundaries facilitate authentic relationships; walls substitute for the vulnerability real connection requires.

Boundaries vs. Demands

- Boundaries focus on what you will do; demands focus on what others must do.
- Boundaries take responsibility for your own limits; demands attempt to control others.
- Boundaries can be maintained regardless of others' responses; demands require others' compliance.

Boundaries vs. Preferences

- Boundaries protect essential needs and values; preferences are about desires and wishes.
- Boundaries involve significant consequences when violated; preferences involve minor disappointment.
- Boundaries are non-negotiable in specific contexts; preferences are flexible.

This clarification helps distinguish true boundary-setting from both rigid isolation and controlling behavior, both of which undermine rather than support authentic connection.

The Roots of Boundary Challenges: Developmental Foundations

Boundary difficulties rarely emerge from nowhere. Most often, they're rooted in early experiences that shaped your understanding of relationships and personal limits:

- **Family system patterns:** Growing up in environments where boundaries were either rigid, nonexistent, or inconsistent.
- **Caretaker reversal:** Having to attend to adults' emotional needs as a child, creating confusion about appropriate responsibilities.
- **Conditional acceptance:** Receiving love and approval only when meeting others' needs or expectations.
- **Trauma history:** Experiencing boundary violations that created fear around self-protection.
- **Cultural messaging:** Absorbing societal or community values that discouraged healthy limits.

Understanding these roots brings compassion to your boundary journey, recognizing that challenges in this area reflect adaptations to your particular history rather than personal failings.

The Boundary Spectrum: Finding Your Balance

Boundaries exist on a spectrum from rigid to porous, with healthy boundaries falling in the flexible middle range:

Rigid Boundaries

- Keeping most people at a distance regardless of context.
- Minimal sharing of feelings or personal information.
- Difficulty asking for help even when appropriate.
- Extreme self-sufficiency that prevents interdependence.
- Black-and-white thinking about relationship rules.

Open Boundaries

- Overinvolvement in others' problems and emotions.
- Difficulty distinguishing your feelings from others'.
- Excessive fear of rejection for saying no.
- Accepting mistreatment to maintain relationships.
- Taking excessive responsibility for others' feelings.

Flexible Boundaries

- Context-sensitive openness appropriate to each relationship.

- Clear sense of responsibility for your emotions and others for theirs.
- Ability to be both connected and separate.
- Comfort with appropriate vulnerability without oversharing.
- Capacity to adjust limits based on trust and safety.

It's true, we each tend to gravitate towards either rigid or porous boundaries, shaped by our past experiences and inherent personalities. Some of us build walls, afraid of vulnerability, while others blur lines, seeking connection at the cost of our own needs. However, the pursuit isn't about achieving a mythical, static "perfect balance" in every single moment. That's unrealistic and, frankly, exhausting. Instead, the real growth lies in cultivating a flexible range, a dynamic ability to adjust your boundaries like a dial, responding to the unique demands of each situation. Finding this healthy balance is a journey of self-discovery. It's about learning to discern when to open up, when to protect, and when to find that sweet spot in between.

Recognizing Boundary Needs

Before you can set effective boundaries, you need to recognize when they're needed. Many people have become so accustomed to boundary violations that they miss the signals indicating a limit has been crossed.

Physical Cues of Boundary Violations: Your Body's Wisdom

Your body often recognizes boundary violations before your conscious mind does, sending physical signals that something isn't right:

- Tension in specific areas (jaw, shoulders, stomach, throat).
- Shallow breathing or breath-holding.
- Restlessness or inability to sit still.
- Sudden fatigue or energy drain.
- Changes in heart rate or body temperature.
- Desire to physically retreat or create distance.

These physical responses aren't random—they're your nervous system's way of alerting you to threats to your psychological safety. Learning to notice these signals early provides valuable information about when boundaries are needed.

Emotional Indicators: Feelings That Signal Boundary Issues

Specific emotional patterns often indicate boundary problems that require attention:

- **Resentment:** Often signals you've agreed to something that violates your values or needs.

- **Guilt without clear wrongdoing:** May indicate you've internalized responsibility for others' emotions.
- **Persistent anxiety in specific relationships:** Can reflect unclear or inconsistent boundaries.
- **Overwhelm:** Often occurs when others' needs consistently override your own.
- **Emptiness after social interaction:** May signal one-way emotional giving without reciprocity.

These emotions aren't problems to eliminate but information to heed, pointing toward areas where clearer boundaries would support your emotional wellbeing.

Energy Assessment: Noticing Relationship Patterns

Another approach to recognizing boundary needs involves assessing the energy flow in your relationships and activities:

- Which interactions leave you feeling energized versus depleted?
- Are there people with whom you consistently feel drained afterward?
- Do certain types of requests or situations create immediate energy drops?
- Are there relationships with consistently one-sided energy exchange?
- Do you experience energy shifts when particular topics arise?

These energy patterns provide valuable data about where boundaries might be needed, highlighting relationships or situations that currently require more from you than they return.

Value Alignment Check: When Boundaries Protect What Matters

Some of the most important boundaries protect your core values from compromise or violation. Checking for value alignment helps identify these boundary needs:

- What activities or requests conflict with your fundamental values?
- Where do you feel pressure to act in ways that contradict your beliefs?
- In what situations do you find yourself compromising what matters most to you?
- Which relationships seem to require setting aside your principles?
- What areas of life create internal conflict between actions and values?

These value conflicts often indicate not just preference differences but essential boundary needs that protect your integrity and authentic self-expression.

Resentment as Information: The Gift of Uncomfortable Feelings

Resentment—often viewed as a negative emotion to overcome—actually provides valuable boundary information when approached with curiosity:

- Persistent resentment usually indicates a boundary has been crossed.
- The intensity of resentment often reflects the importance of the boundary violated.
- Recurring resentment in similar situations reveals pattern recognition.
- The specific focus of resentment points toward the exact boundary needed.
- Resolution of resentment typically requires boundary setting rather than just attitude adjustment.

Learning to view resentment as information rather than a character flaw transforms it from a problem into a resource for identifying boundary needs.

Setting and Communicating Boundaries

Once you've recognized where boundaries are needed, the next challenge involves actually establishing and expressing them effectively.

The Anatomy of a Clear Boundary: Essential Components

Effective boundaries typically include several key elements:

- **Clear limits:** Specific description of what is and isn't acceptable.
- **Personal ownership:** Framing the boundary as your need rather than others' failing.
- **Consequences:** What will happen if the boundary is crossed.
- **Positive intent:** What the boundary protects or makes possible.
- **Implementation plan:** How you'll maintain the boundary in practice.

Including these components creates boundaries that are both clear to others and sustainable for you to maintain.

Language Templates: Specific Phrases for Different Scenarios

Having specific language ready for common boundary situations reduces the stress of in-the-moment formulation. These templates can be adapted to your particular circumstances:

For time boundaries:

- "I can give you 15 minutes now, and then I need to return to my work."
- "I'm not available at that time, but I could meet on Tuesday afternoon."
- "I'll need to leave by 9:00 to honor my commitment to getting sufficient rest."

For emotional boundaries:

- "I care about your situation, but I'm not in a position to take responsibility for solving it."

- "I need some time to process my own feelings before discussing this further."
- "I understand you're upset, and those feelings make sense. I'm not taking them on as something I need to fix."

For physical/personal space boundaries:

- "I'm someone who needs advance notice before social visits."
- "I'm not comfortable with that level of physical contact in our relationship."
- "My personal belongings are important to me, and I need you to ask before borrowing them."

For information boundaries:

- "That's not something I'm comfortable discussing."
- "I appreciate your interest, but that's private information for me."
- "I'll share more about that when I feel ready."

These templates provide starting points that you can modify to fit your authentic voice and specific situations.

Non-verbal Boundary Setting: Body Language and Environmental Boundaries

Not all boundaries require verbal expression. Non-verbal and environmental boundaries can be equally effective in certain contexts:

Body language boundaries:

- Physical distance that communicates comfort level.
- Hand gestures that signal "stop" or "enough".
- Facial expressions that convey limits being reached.
- Posture shifts that create more personal space.
- Eye contact changes that regulate conversational intimacy.

Environmental boundaries:

- Creating physical spaces that reflect your needs for privacy.
- Using headphones to signal unavailability for conversation.
- Closing doors to indicate need for uninterrupted time.
- Arranging furniture to facilitate comfortable interaction distance.
- Using do-not-disturb signs or signals in shared spaces.

These non-verbal boundaries often work effectively for day-to-day situations, reserving more direct verbal boundary setting for significant or persistent issues.

> "Boundaries are to protect life, not to limit pleasures." - Edwin Louis Cole.

GRADUATED RESPONSES: ESCALATING BOUNDARY REINFORCEMENT WHEN NEEDED

Not all boundary violations require the same level of response. Having a graduated approach allows you to match your response to the situation:

Level 1: Gentle reminder

- Subtle non-verbal cues.
- Brief, non-confrontational verbal reminders.
- Light redirection to alternative behaviors.

Level 2: Clear restatement

- More explicit verbal boundary statements.
- Firmer tone while maintaining respect.
- Direct connection between behavior and boundary.

Level 3: Boundary with consequences

- Clear statement of what will happen if boundary continues to be crossed.
- Implementation of natural consequences.
- Limit-setting on the relationship itself if needed.

Level 4: Enforced distance

- Creating physical or emotional space from persistent boundary violations.
- Involving others for support when appropriate.
- Formal limits on engagement.

This graduated approach prevents the common pattern of saying nothing until you reach a breaking point, then responding with an intensity that seems disproportionate to others.

> "When you say 'yes' to others, make sure you are not saying 'no' to yourself." - Paulo Coelho.

BOUNDARY-SETTING REHEARSAL: PRACTICING DIFFICULT CONVERSATIONS IN ADVANCE

For important or challenging boundary conversations, rehearsal significantly increases effectiveness:

- Script key points you want to convey clearly.
- Practice with a supportive person who can provide feedback.
- Anticipate potential responses and plan how you'll address them.
- Work with body sensations that arise during rehearsal.
- Identify support resources for before and after the conversation.

This rehearsal isn't about creating a rigid script but about developing familiarity with the territory so you can stay present and authentic during the actual conversation.

MAINTAINING BOUNDARIES OVER TIME

Setting boundaries is just the beginning—maintaining them consistently over time presents its own challenges and requires specific skills.

CONSISTENCY CHALLENGES: WHY BOUNDARIES OFTEN ERODE

Several factors commonly contribute to boundary erosion over time:

- **Guilt resurgence:** Renewed feelings of selfishness or responsibility for others' reactions.
- **Path of least resistance:** Short-term ease of compliance versus long-term cost of boundary violations.
- **Intermittent reinforcement:** Occasional positive responses to boundary relaxation.
- **Relationship pressure:** Direct or indirect pushback from others.
- **Internal belief challenges:** Resurfacing of old messages about your right to have needs.

Recognizing these common erosion patterns helps you anticipate and prepare for the challenges of boundary maintenance rather than being surprised when they emerge.

> **"Part of courage is simple consistency." - Peggy Noonan.**

MANAGING GUILT AND DISCOMFORT: WORKING WITH DIFFICULT EMOTIONS DURING BOUNDARY PRACTICE

Uncomfortable emotions—particularly guilt—frequently arise when maintaining boundaries, especially with people unaccustomed to your limits. Approaches for working with these feelings include:

- Recognizing guilt doesn't mean you're doing anything wrong.
- Distinguishing between genuine wrongdoing and conditioned people-pleasing.
- Having self-compassion statements ready for difficult moments.
- Connecting to the values your boundaries protect.
- Seeking support from people who affirm your right to have boundaries.

This emotional work is often the most challenging aspect of boundary maintenance, requiring as much attention as the external boundary communication itself.

Boundary Adjustments: Recalibrating as Needs and Relationships Change

Healthy boundaries aren't static—they evolve as you and your relationships develop:

- Periodically reassessing whether current boundaries still serve their purpose.
- Being willing to loosen boundaries when greater trust has been established.
- Strengthening boundaries in areas where violations have occurred.
- Adapting boundaries to major life transitions and role changes.
- Developing more nuanced, context-specific boundaries over time.

This flexibility prevents boundaries from becoming rigid rules disconnected from their original protective purpose, allowing them to remain living expressions of your current needs and values.

By practicing self-awareness and self-regulation, you learn to navigate the emotional landscape of boundary-setting with greater confidence and compassion, transforming difficult emotions from obstacles into opportunities for growth and deeper self-understanding. You are cultivating the strength to stand in your truth, and that strength is a powerful expression of your authentic self.

Recovery from Boundary Violations: Steps to Take When Lines Are Crossed

Even well-established boundaries sometimes get crossed. Having a recovery process helps you respond effectively rather than either overreacting or abandoning the boundary:

1. **Acknowledge the violation:** Recognize what happened without minimization.
2. **Check internal impact:** Notice your emotional and physical response.
3. **Assess intent vs. impact:** Consider whether the violation was intentional or accidental.
4. **Reaffirm the boundary:** Clearly restate your limit if appropriate.
5. **Implement consequences:** Follow through with any previously stated outcomes.
6. **Evaluate patterns:** Note whether this is an isolated incident or part of a pattern.

7. **Practice self-care:** Attend to any emotional aftermath.
8. **Consider adjustments:** Determine if the boundary needs strengthening or clarification.

This structured approach prevents boundary violations from either derailing your practice entirely or accumulating without response.

COMMUNITY SUPPORT: CREATING ENVIRONMENTS THAT REINFORCE HEALTHY BOUNDARIES

Maintaining boundaries becomes significantly easier within supportive communities. Approaches for creating this support include:

- Spending more time with people who respect and model healthy boundaries.
- Explicitly discussing boundary norms in important relationships.
- Creating mutual agreements in family or work systems about respect for limits.
- Sharing your boundary journey with trusted others who can provide accountability.
- Seeking communities (therapy groups, workshops, spiritual communities) that explicitly value boundaries.

This social reinforcement creates an environment where your boundaries are supported rather than constantly challenged, making maintenance substantially easier. Seeking out communities that value authenticity, respect, and clear communication can significantly reinforce your boundary-setting efforts. Sharing your experiences with trusted individuals can normalize the challenges you face and provide valuable insights and encouragement.

THE JOURNEY OF BOUNDARY DEVELOPMENT

The journey of boundary development is a dynamic, evolving process, not a static endpoint. It's similar to learning a new language; you start with basic phrases, gradually expanding your vocabulary and fluency over time. This journey requires patience and self-forgiveness, as you'll inevitably encounter moments of uncertainty and missteps. Treat each interaction as a learning opportunity, observing the impact of your boundaries and adjusting them accordingly. Embrace the fact that your needs will change, and your boundaries must adapt to reflect your growth. This continuous refinement is a testament to your commitment to self-respect and authentic living.

Developing healthy boundaries is rarely a linear process. Most people experience cycles of clarity and confusion, strength and surrender, as they learn this essential skill. What matters isn't perfect boundary maintenance but ongoing commitment to honoring your authentic needs even through inevitable setbacks.

Remember that boundary setting isn't selfish—it's an act of integrity that benefits not just you but everyone in your life. Clear boundaries prevent the resentment, confusion, and passive aggression that poison relationships, creating instead the safety that allows genuine intimacy to flourish.

As you continue strengthening your boundary practice, you'll likely notice an unexpected paradox: the clearer your boundaries become, the more freely you can experience authentic connection. When you no longer fear being engulfed or controlled by others, you can risk the vulnerability that deep relationship requires.

In the next section, we'll explore this vulnerability directly, examining its essential role in authentic living and how to practice it wisely within the protective framework of healthy boundaries.

The Role of Vulnerability in Authenticity

Embracing vulnerability requires a shift in perspective. It's about recognizing that imperfection is not a flaw but a shared human experience that binds us together. It's about understanding that true strength lies not in hiding our weaknesses but in having the courage to share them. This practice of vulnerability is not about oversharing or seeking validation, but about creating space for genuine connection and fostering a sense of belonging. It's a powerful act of self-acceptance and self-compassion, signaling to yourself and others that you are worthy of love and connection, just as you are.

The Courage to Be Seen

After exploring mindfulness for awareness, communication strategies for expression, and boundaries for protection, we come to perhaps the most challenging aspect of emotional authenticity: vulnerability—the willingness to be genuinely seen, with all your imperfections and uncertainties intact.

Vulnerability often triggers fear. We worry that showing our true selves—including our doubts, struggles, and imperfections—will lead to rejection, judgment, or exploitation. Yet without this willingness to be seen authentically, we remain hidden behind masks of perfection or indifference that prevent genuine connection both with others and with ourselves.

Reframing Vulnerability as Strength

Our cultural understanding of vulnerability often equates it with weakness or risk. To practice authentic vulnerability requires fundamentally reframing this concept, recognizing it as a form of courage rather than a form of exposure.

The Vulnerability Paradox: Strength Through Openness

One of the most powerful paradoxes of emotional life is that authentic vulnerability—far from making you weaker—actually creates a deeper form of strength. This paradox becomes clear when we consider the alternatives:

- The person who never admits mistakes lives in constant fear of being discovered.
- The leader who can't acknowledge uncertainty must waste energy maintaining an illusion of perfect knowledge.
- The partner who hides feelings requires enormous effort to maintain emotional walls.
- The friend who never asks for help carries burdens alone unnecessarily.

Each of these invulnerable postures creates a brittle form of strength that requires constant maintenance and remains perpetually at risk of collapse. In contrast, the willingness to be authentically seen—including your limitations, needs, and uncertainties—creates a resilient strength based on truth rather than performance.

"Being vulnerable is the only way to allow your heart to feel true pleasure." - Bob Marley.

Research consistently confirms this paradox. Studies show that people who practice appropriate vulnerability experience:

- Greater emotional resilience during challenges.
- Stronger and more satisfying relationships.
- Reduced anxiety about being "found out" or rejected.
- Higher ratings of perceived authenticity from others.
- Increased access to social support during difficulties.

This research affirms what many discover through experience: the courage to be authentically seen creates a foundation far stronger than any protective armor.

Distinguishing Healthy Vulnerability from Oversharing

An important clarification: authentic vulnerability is not the same as indiscriminate sharing of personal information. The distinction involves several key factors:

Healthy vulnerability:

- Is offered with discernment about context and relationship.
- Serves connection rather than attention-seeking.
- Respects appropriate boundaries.

- Comes from a centered rather than desperate place.
- Includes awareness of potential impact on others.

Unhealthy oversharing:

- Lacks contextual appropriateness or relationship readiness.
- Often serves unconscious needs for validation or rescue.
- Ignores boundaries—both yours and others'.
- Frequently comes from emotional flooding or neediness.
- May overwhelm listeners or create uncomfortable obligations.

This distinction helps clarify that authentic vulnerability isn't about emotional dumping but about thoughtful revelation of your truth in service of genuine connection.

Healthy vulnerability is about selective, intentional sharing that builds connection and fosters intimacy, not a blanket broadcast of every thought and feeling. It's the art of discerning who is safe and trustworthy, and then choosing to reveal aspects of yourself that create genuine understanding and mutual respect. Oversharing, on the other hand, often stems from a need for validation or attention, blurring boundaries and potentially leaving you feeling exposed and depleted.

CULTURAL AND GENDER INFLUENCES: NAVIGATING SOCIAL MESSAGES

Our comfort with vulnerability is profoundly shaped by cultural and gender expectations that begin in early childhood. These influences create specific challenges that require awareness:

Cultural variations:

- Some cultures highly value emotional restraint and self-containment.
- Others encourage expressive communication but limit which emotions are acceptable.
- Family cultural norms often overlay broader societal expectations.
- Professional cultures create their own rules about appropriate vulnerability.
- Generational differences influence vulnerability norms.

Gendered expectations:

- Many men are socialized to view vulnerability as weakness.
- Many women are taught to be emotionally open but not to express "negative" emotions like anger.
- Nonbinary and gender-nonconforming people often navigate complex, contradictory expectations.
- Different aspects of vulnerability (emotional, physical, financial) carry different gendered scripts.

These cultural and gender patterns aren't destiny, but acknowledging their influence helps explain internal resistance to vulnerability that might otherwise be confusing. Understanding these patterns allows you to make conscious choices about which inherited norms serve your authentic expression and which constrain it unnecessarily.

The Courage Equation: Vulnerability Plus Boundaries

Perhaps the most empowering reframe of vulnerability comes from understanding its relationship to boundaries. Authentic vulnerability isn't unlimited exposure but rather chosen openness within appropriate boundaries.

This relationship can be expressed as a simple equation: **Vulnerability + Boundaries = Courage**

Without boundaries, vulnerability becomes unsafe exposure. Without vulnerability, boundaries create isolation rather than connection. Together, they create the conditions for genuine courage—the willingness to risk being seen while maintaining the self-respect of clear limits.

Examples of this integration include:

- Sharing feelings about a conflict while maintaining boundaries about respectful discussion.
- Admitting a mistake at work while being clear about unfair criticism.
- Expressing needs in a relationship while respecting that they may not always be met.
- Revealing fears or insecurities while not making others responsible for managing them.
- Being open about struggles while maintaining appropriate privacy around details.

This balanced approach transforms vulnerability from a feared risk to a chosen practice of authentic engagement.

Research Findings: Evidence of Vulnerability's Benefits

The benefits of appropriate vulnerability are more than theoretical—a substantial body of research confirms its positive impacts:

- **Connection studies:** Appropriate self-disclosure consistently predicts relationship satisfaction and depth.
- **Leadership research:** Leaders who show authentic vulnerability are rated as more trustworthy and effective.
- **Health outcomes:** People who practice emotional openness show better immune function and longevity.
- **Mental health findings:** Appropriate vulnerability correlates with lower rates of depression and anxiety.
- **Workplace studies:** Teams with psychological safety (ability to be vulnerable) consistently outperform those without it.

Vulnerability, when practiced with discernment, unlocks a wealth of profound benefits: it deepens connection by fostering trust and intimacy, it strengthens self-acceptance by normalizing imperfection, it builds resilience by allowing us to process difficult emotions, and it cultivates authenticity by aligning our inner and outer selves, ultimately leading to a more meaningful and fulfilling life.

"What happens when people open their hearts? They get better." - Haruki Murakami.

THE VULNERABILITY PROGRESSION

Like any skill, vulnerability develops through practice rather than theory. Most people benefit from a progressive approach that gradually expands comfort with being authentically seen.

STARTING WITH SAFER CONTEXTS: STRATEGIC VULNERABILITY

Beginning your vulnerability practice in carefully chosen contexts creates successful experiences that build confidence:

- **Trustworthy individuals:** People who have demonstrated respect for your feelings.
- **Structured settings:** Support groups, therapy, or workshops designed for authentic sharing.
- **Clear agreements:** Relationships with explicit understandings about confidentiality and respect.
- **Reciprocal relationships:** Connections where vulnerability flows in both directions.
- **Lower-stakes content:** Topics that carry emotional significance but not overwhelming charge.

These safer contexts allow you to experience the benefits of being authentically seen while minimizing the risks that make vulnerability frightening.

BUILDING THE VULNERABILITY MUSCLE: GRADUAL EXPANSION

As your comfort with vulnerability grows in safer contexts, you can gradually expand your practice:

- **Content progression:** Moving from sharing preferences to feelings to deeper needs and fears.
- **Context expansion:** Practicing vulnerability in a wider range of relationships and settings.
- **Recovery development:** Building resilience when vulnerability isn't met as hoped.
- **Timing variation:** Moving from carefully planned vulnerability to more spontaneous authenticity.
- **Integration into identity:** Shifting from "doing vulnerability" to incorporating it as part of who you are.

This gradual progression prevents the common pattern of avoiding vulnerability entirely or diving into overwhelming exposure that triggers retreat back into protective armor.

Discernment Practices: Choosing What, When, Where, and With Whom

Effective vulnerability requires discernment—the wisdom to assess which aspects of yourself to share in which contexts. This isn't about being inauthentic but about recognizing that context matters for meaningful connection.

Factors to consider in vulnerability decisions include:

- **Relationship history:** The established trust and patterns in this specific connection.
- **Purpose:** What genuine connection might be served by this sharing.
- **Timing:** Whether this is an appropriate moment for vulnerable exchange.
- **Capacity:** Both your emotional resources and the other person's current bandwidth.
- **Content appropriateness:** Whether the vulnerability fits the relationship context

This discernment isn't calculated manipulation but thoughtful consideration that honors both your needs and the realities of different relationships and contexts.

Recovery Skills: Handling When Vulnerability Isn't Received Well

Even with careful discernment, sometimes vulnerability isn't met with the understanding or respect we hope for. Having recovery skills prevents these difficult experiences from shutting down your willingness to be authentic:

- **Self-validation:** Affirming the courage it took regardless of the response.
- **Context evaluation:** Assessing whether this relationship is generally supportive of authenticity.
- **Response separation:** Distinguishing between the other person's reaction and your worth.
- **Appropriate responsibility:** Taking ownership of your expression without taking blame for others' reactions.
- **Support activation:** Reaching out to understanding others after difficult vulnerability experiences.

Think of recovery skills as your emotional safety net, turning vulnerability from a tightrope walk into a dance where missteps are part of the choreography. They're the tools that allow you to lean into vulnerability, knowing you have the means to gently guide yourself back to equilibrium. These skills—like self-soothing, boundary setting, and mindful acknowledgment—transform vulnerability from a high-stakes gamble into a practice you can engage in imperfectly while continuing to learn and grow.

The Authenticity Feedback Loop: How Vulnerability Reinforces Authentic Living

As you practice vulnerability consistently, a positive feedback loop often develops that reinforces authentic living:

1. Vulnerability allows you to be seen more authentically.
2. Being authentically seen creates deeper connection.
3. Deeper connection provides support for continued authenticity.
4. This support makes further vulnerability feel safer.
5. Safer vulnerability allows even deeper authenticity to emerge.

This virtuous cycle gradually transforms vulnerability from a frightening challenge to a natural way of being that creates the connection and support that sustains authentic living.

Vulnerability in Different Relationships

Vulnerability manifests differently across various relationship contexts, each with its own opportunities and challenges for authentic expression. The key is to calibrate your vulnerability to the context and the relationship's dynamic, prioritizing trust, mutual respect, and clear communication to ensure that your openness fosters connection rather than creating discomfort or exploitation.

Intimate Partnerships: The Special Role of Vulnerability in Close Relationships

Romantic partnerships often involve the deepest vulnerability, creating both the greatest potential for connection and the most significant risks:

- **Emotional vulnerability:** Sharing your full range of feelings, including difficult ones.
- **Historical vulnerability:** Revealing formative experiences and wounds.
- **Need vulnerability:** Expressing genuine desires and requirements.
- **Physical vulnerability:** Being authentically seen and known in bodily intimacy.
- **Dream vulnerability:** Sharing hopes and aspirations that matter deeply.

The depth of potential vulnerability in partnerships makes thoughtful progression particularly important. Many relationships benefit from explicitly discussing comfort levels and gradually expanding vulnerable sharing as trust develops.

FRIENDSHIPS: BUILDING DEPTH THROUGH APPROPRIATE VULNERABILITY

Friendship provides a crucial context for vulnerability that differs from romantic relationships:

- Less expectation of complete sharing creates more selective vulnerability.
- Often provides more diverse perspectives than partner relationships.
- May offer longer historical context for vulnerability due to relationship longevity.
- Typically involves fewer practical entanglements, potentially creating safer space.
- Different friendships may support different aspects of vulnerable expression.

The diversity of friendship connections allows for a portfolio approach to vulnerability—sharing different aspects of yourself with friends whose particular strengths, perspectives, or experiences create resonance with specific parts of your authentic self.

FAMILY DYNAMICS: NAVIGATING VULNERABILITY IN COMPLEX HISTORICAL RELATIONSHIPS

Family relationships present unique vulnerability challenges due to their long history and established patterns:

- Childhood roles and expectations often persist into adult relationships.
- Historical wounds may complicate present vulnerability.
- Family culture creates strong norms about emotional expression.
- Power dynamics from earlier life stages may still influence interactions.
- Shared history provides both connection opportunities and potential triggers.

These complexities require especially thoughtful vulnerability practice, often beginning with smaller authentic expressions to test how they're received before moving toward deeper sharing. In some cases, family relationships may not currently support authentic vulnerability, requiring acceptance of these limitations while seeking expression in more receptive contexts.

> **"Being vulnerable means being open, for wounding, but also for pleasure." - Robin S. Sharma.**

PROFESSIONAL CONTEXTS: STRATEGIC AUTHENTICITY IN WORKPLACE SETTINGS

Work environments typically have different vulnerability norms than personal relationships, requiring thoughtful navigation:

- Power dynamics influence what authentic expression feels safe.
- Professional expectations create contextual boundaries around appropriate sharing.
- Vulnerability about relevant limitations often builds rather than diminishes credibility.
- Workplace cultures vary dramatically in their support for authentic expression.
- Strategic vulnerability focuses on aspects that serve team functions and relationship building.

The key in professional contexts is discerning what aspects of vulnerability serve both authentic expression and appropriate workplace functioning, recognizing that authenticity doesn't require sharing every aspect of yourself in all contexts.

COMMUNITY CONNECTIONS: BUILDING GENUINE BELONGING THROUGH SHARED VULNERABILITY

Beyond individual relationships, community contexts offer unique opportunities for vulnerability that creates genuine belonging:

- Shared values provide foundation for authentic expression.
- Collective vulnerability often emerges around common experiences or challenges.
- Rituals and traditions may create containers for meaningful vulnerability.
- Multiple relationships offer diverse connections for different aspects of authenticity.
- Community norms can either support or inhibit vulnerable expression.

Authenticity, while an internal journey, flourishes within the fertile soil of a supportive community. It's about recognizing that we are not solitary islands, but interconnected beings who thrive on genuine connection. A community that values vulnerability, celebrates individuality, and encourages honest expression acts as a powerful mirror, reflecting back our truest selves. Within such a space, the fear of judgment diminishes, replaced by a sense of belonging and acceptance. This allows us to shed the masks we wear for self-preservation and embrace the courage to be seen and heard. Sharing our struggles, celebrating our triumphs, and receiving compassionate feedback creates a collective container for growth, where authenticity is not only encouraged but becomes the natural language of connection. This shared experience reinforces our commitment to living genuinely, reminding us that we are not alone on this path, and that our authentic selves are both valued and necessary.

VULNERABILITY WITH YOURSELF: THE INTERNAL DIMENSION

While we often think of vulnerability primarily in relational contexts, perhaps the most fundamental vulnerability involves being honest with yourself about aspects of your experience that challenge your self-concept or comfort.

Internal Resistance to Self-Knowledge: Common Patterns of Self-Deception

Most people maintain areas of strategic blindness—aspects of themselves they unconsciously avoid seeing clearly. Common patterns include:

- **Defense against pain:** Avoiding awareness of wounds, grief, or trauma.
- **Protection of self-image:** Resisting recognition of traits that contradict how you want to see yourself.
- **Disowned desires:** Suppressing awareness of wants that seem inappropriate or unattainable.
- **Inconvenient truths:** Avoiding acknowledgment of realities that might require difficult changes.
- **Shadow material:** Denying aspects of yourself that were rejected or shamed in formative experiences.

This internal resistance creates fragmentation—parts of your experience remain excluded from conscious awareness, preventing full authentic presence even with yourself.

Shadow Work: Facing Disowned Aspects of Yourself

Shadow work involves deliberately turning toward the parts of yourself you've disowned or denied—not to judge them, but to integrate them into a more complete self-awareness:

- **Projection recognition:** Noticing when you strongly react to qualities in others you deny in yourself.
- **Dream exploration:** Paying attention to dream symbols that may represent disowned aspects.
- **Triggered awareness:** Using emotional triggers as gateways to shadow material.
- **Guided journaling:** Writing from the perspective of rejected parts of yourself.
- **Safe accompaniment:** Working with a therapist or guide when exploring challenging shadow material.

This work requires internal vulnerability—the willingness to acknowledge aspects of yourself that don't fit your preferred self-image or that carry shame or judgment.

Self-Forgiveness Practices: Coming to Terms with Mistakes and Regrets

Another dimension of internal vulnerability involves honest acknowledgment of mistakes, regrets, and failures—not to indulge in self-criticism but to allow genuine reconciliation with your imperfect humanity:

- **Specific acknowledgment:** Naming exactly what you regret without minimization or exaggeration

- **Intention recognition:** Understanding the needs or fears that drove problematic actions
- **Impact honoring:** Fully acknowledging effects on yourself and others
- **Amends consideration:** Identifying appropriate repair where possible
- **Integration practice:** Finding the learning without being defined by past mistakes

This self-forgiveness requires the vulnerability to see yourself clearly without the protection of either denial ("I did nothing wrong") or self-punishment ("I am fundamentally flawed").

Mistakes are the portals of discovery." - James Joyce.

DREAMS AND ASPIRATIONS: THE VULNERABILITY OF ACKNOWLEDGING DEEPER DESIRES

Perhaps surprisingly, acknowledging your deepest dreams and aspirations requires significant vulnerability—opening to potential disappointment and recognizing desires that may seem too big or unlikely:

- **Permission to want:** Allowing yourself to acknowledge what you truly desire.
- **Beyond practicality:** Connecting with dreams regardless of their apparent feasibility.
- **Desire without guarantee:** Opening to wanting without certainty of fulfillment.
- **Identity expansion:** Recognizing aspirations that challenge your current self-concept.
- **Worthiness claims:** Affirming that your dreams matter regardless of external validation.

This vulnerability with your own deeper desires creates the possibility for life choices aligned with your authentic values rather than constrained by fear or artificial limitation.

"The future belongs to those who believe in the beauty of their dreams." - Eleanor Roosevelt.

IDENTITY EVOLUTION: THE COURAGE TO OUTGROW FORMER VERSIONS OF YOURSELF

A final dimension of internal vulnerability involves allowing your sense of self to evolve—recognizing when you've outgrown former identities, beliefs, or patterns that once felt central to who you are:

- **Belief revision:** Acknowledging when perspectives that once seemed certain no longer ring true.
- **Role transformation:** Recognizing when familiar roles no longer fit your authentic self.
- **Value clarification:** Allowing your core values to evolve with experience and growth.
- **Potential emergence:** Opening to capabilities and qualities previously not associated with your identity.

- **Past-self compassion:** Holding former versions of yourself with understanding rather than judgment.

Look, we've all got those old versions of ourselves hanging around, right? Like, that person we used to be, maybe the one who always played it safe, or the one who tried to please everyone. But here's the thing: you're not stuck with that person. You're allowed to change, to grow, to outgrow those old skins. It takes guts, though, because it means saying goodbye to what's familiar, even if it wasn't serving you. It's like, you're looking in the mirror and saying, "Thanks for getting me this far, old me, but I'm moving on now.

And yes, it can feel weird, even a little scary. People might look at you funny, wondering where the "old you" went. But that's okay. You're not doing this for them; you're doing it for you. It's about giving yourself permission to evolve, to become the person you were always meant to be. It's about realizing that your identity isn't fixed, it's a living, breathing thing that's constantly changing. And when you embrace that change, when you have the courage to shed those old layers, you'll find a freedom and authenticity you never knew existed. You're not losing yourself; you're finding yourself. This vulnerability allows your identity to remain a living, evolving expression of your authentic self rather than a fixed definition that constrains your growth and expression.

> **"I prefer to be true to myself, even at the hazard of incurring the ridicule of others, rather than to be false, and to incur my own abhorrence." - Frederick Douglass.**

THE INTEGRATION OF AUTHENTICITY PRACTICES

As we conclude this chapter on practices for emotional authenticity, it's important to recognize how these different approaches—mindfulness, communication, boundaries, and vulnerability—work together as an integrated system rather than isolated techniques.

Mindfulness creates the awareness that makes authentic communication possible. Boundaries provide the safety that allows vulnerability to flourish. Vulnerability creates the connection that makes authentic communication meaningful. Each practice supports and enhances the others in a synergistic relationship.

This integration extends beyond techniques to the fundamental purpose of emotional authenticity—not self-improvement or relationship enhancement, though these often result, but the simple yet profound experience of being fully present with your own life, inhabiting your experience without the exhausting mediations of performance, pretense, or protection.

Reflection Questions

1. In this moment, what am I truly feeling, and what does that feeling need from me? (This focuses on self-awareness and self-regulation, encouraging you to connect with your emotions and respond with compassion.)
2. If I were to act from my most authentic self right now, what would I say or do differently? (This prompts you to identify any discrepancies between your current behavior and your true values, pushing you towards authentic expression.)
3. What boundaries do I need to establish or reinforce to honor my emotional well-being in this situation? (This directs your attention to boundary setting, encouraging you to prioritize your needs and create healthy relational dynamics.)
4. How can I bring more mindful presence to this interaction, allowing me to truly connect with myself and others? (This emphasizes the importance of mindfulness and empathy, fostering genuine connection and social awareness.)
5. Looking back on this interaction, where did I feel most authentic, and where did I compromise myself? What can I learn from this?" (This encourages reflection and continuous learning, helping them refine their authentic practices and integrate them into their daily life).

Chapter 5: Taking One Day at a Time: Integrating Authentic Living into Your Daily Life

Understanding authenticity is one thing. Living it consistently in the messy reality of everyday life is entirely another. By now, you've explored the distinction between your authentic and conditioned selves. You've learned about the alignment process and specific practices for emotional authenticity. But let's be real, life throws curveballs. Deadlines, drama, those old habits creeping back in – it's a messy business. In today's world, where everything's fast-paced and demanding, how do you actually live this stuff? The key is to take it one day, even one moment, at a time. Forget about some grand, overnight transformation. Start small. Before you hit "send" on that email, take a breath and ask, "Is this really me talking?" When that old people-pleasing urge kicks in, try saying a gentle "no" and see what happens. It's about tiny, conscious choices, sprinkled throughout your day. You're not aiming for perfection, just a little more realness, a little more often. And when you slip up, because you will, don't beat yourself up. Just notice, adjust, and keep going. This isn't a race; it's a marathon. You're building new habits, one breath, one boundary, one honest word at a time.

This is where the rubber meets the road—where inspiring concepts become lived experience or slowly fade into the category of "good ideas I once read about." The difference lies not in momentary motivation but in practical integration.

Creating Supportive Environments for Authentic Living

Your Surroundings Shape Your Authenticity

The journey toward emotional alignment doesn't happen in a vacuum. Your physical spaces, social circles, time structures, and information inputs all profoundly influence your capacity for authentic living. While internal practices form the foundation of emotional authenticity, external environments either reinforce or undermine these efforts.

Think of your environment as the soil in which your authentic self grows. Even the strongest plant struggles in poor soil, while even a vulnerable seedling thrives in nourishing ground. By intentionally shaping your surroundings to support authenticity, you reduce the friction in your alignment journey and create conditions where being your true self becomes the path of least resistance rather than constant struggle.

Physical Spaces That Support Authenticity

The physical environments you inhabit affect your emotional state, sense of identity, and capacity for authentic presence in ways both obvious and subtle. With thoughtful attention, you can transform your spaces to actively support your authentic expression.

Home Environment Design: Your Authentic Sanctuary

Your home is the environment over which you typically have the most control, making it the natural place to begin creating spaces that reflect and nurture your authentic self:

- **Personal expression:** Surround yourself with objects, colors, and images that genuinely resonate rather than following external trends or expectations. What truly brings you joy or peace when you see it daily?
- **Emotional needs assessment:** Different authentic emotions require different types of support. Consider creating distinct zones in your home: spaces that energize, spaces that calm, spaces that inspire creativity, and spaces that facilitate connection.
- **Sensory alignment:** Notice which sensory experiences support your authentic presence. This might include particular music, scents, textures, or lighting that help you feel more genuinely yourself.
- **Boundary reinforcement:** Design features that support your need for privacy and solitude balanced with spaces that welcome connection when desired. Physical boundaries often support emotional ones.
- **Values reflection:** Ensure your living space reflects what truly matters to you rather than what you think should matter. Is your home arranged around entertainment, creativity, comfort, functionality, aesthetics, or something else? Does this alignment reflect your authentic values?

Even small adjustments can significantly impact how your home environment supports authenticity. One client transformed a crowded desk area into a daily authenticity reminder by simply clearing everything except for a beautiful stone, a small plant, and a handwritten note about her core values. This tiny "authenticity anchor" created a visual reminder of her commitment to aligned living.

> **"If you do not consciously design your environment, it will design you." - Marshall Goldsmith.**

Workplace Adjustments: Bringing Authenticity into Professional Settings

While you may have less control over work environments, strategic modifications can create pockets of authenticity even in conventional settings:

- **Personal workspace elements:** Incorporate small objects or images that quietly remind you of your authentic self, even if they're only visible to you.
- **Nature connection:** Position yourself near windows when possible or bring plants into your workspace to support present-moment awareness.
- **Transition zones:** Create physical or temporal boundaries between work and personal life that help you shift between different authentic expressions rather than carrying work personas home.
- **Communication supports:** Design your space to facilitate the types of interaction that allow your authentic contribution—whether that means creating quiet zones for focused work or collaborative areas for genuine exchange.
- **Values visibility:** Keep reminders of your core values visible in your workspace, perhaps through meaningful quotes, symbols, or images that reconnect you with what matters.

In even the most conventional work settings, these subtle adjustments can create "authenticity anchors" that help you maintain connection to your true self amid external expectations.

Digital Environment Curation: Managing Virtual Spaces

For many of us, digital environments constitute a significant portion of our daily experience, making them crucial territories for authenticity support:

- **Notification management:** Adjust settings to prevent constant interruption of your authentic presence with devices that demand immediate attention.
- **Social media curation:** Consciously select accounts and communities that reinforce rather than undermine your authentic values and self-acceptance.
- **Digital boundaries:** Create clear separations between different digital activities—perhaps using different browsers for work and personal use, or designating specific times for different types of engagement.
- **Visual design:** Customize your digital spaces with images, themes, and organizations that reflect your authentic aesthetic rather than defaults.
- **Intentional absence:** Designate specific technology-free zones or times in your life where direct experience takes precedence over digital mediation.

These digital environment adjustments reduce the cognitive and emotional load of constantly switching between online expectations and authentic presence, creating more coherence in your daily experience.

Sensory Considerations: The Subtle Impact of Perception

Our sensory experiences profoundly affect our emotional state and capacity for authentic presence, often below the threshold of conscious awareness:

- **Lighting quality:** Natural light typically supports emotional awareness, while harsh artificial lighting can trigger stress responses that disconnect you from authentic experience.
- **Sound landscape:** Background noise significantly impacts your nervous system. Notice which sound environments support your authentic presence—whether that's music, natural sounds, productive ambient noise, or silence.
- **Color influence:** Different colors affect mood and energy. Observe which colors help you feel more genuinely yourself and incorporate them strategically in your environments.
- **Tactile experience:** The textures you interact with daily—from clothing to furniture to tools—create subtle but significant impacts on your comfort and groundedness.
- **Air quality:** Proper ventilation, humidity, and freshness support the physical wellbeing that forms the foundation for emotional authenticity.

These sensory factors might seem superficial compared to deeper psychological work, but they create the immediate physical context in which your nervous system operates, directly affecting your capacity for authentic presence.

> **"Perception is not always reality, but it's real to those who perceive it." - Bobby Darnell.**

"Perception is reality" sounds profound, but it's a dangerous oversimplification. Your perception is your reality, a unique and subjective interpretation of the world, filtered through your past experiences, biases, and emotional state. It's a lens, not a mirror. While it shapes how you react and interact, it doesn't erase the objective truth. Two people can witness the same event and have vastly different perceptions, yet the event itself remains unchanged. Understanding this distinction is crucial; it allows for empathy, recognizing that others' realities are valid to them, even if they differ from yours. It also empowers you to question your own perceptions, to seek multiple perspectives, and to strive for a more accurate understanding of the world, rather than blindly accepting your initial impression as the absolute truth.

Decluttering for Clarity: Creating Space for Authenticity

Physical clutter often correlates with emotional and mental clutter, creating noise that drowns out the quieter voice of your authentic self:

- **Possession alignment:** Regularly gauge whether the objects in your environment genuinely support your current authentic values and needs, or remain from past versions of yourself or external expectations.
- **Attention protection:** Reduce visual distractions in spaces where you want to connect more deeply with yourself or others.
- **Decision reduction:** Minimize environments that require constant trivial choices, preserving your decision-making energy for authentic discernment about what truly matters.
- **Transition support:** Create clear entry and exit points in your spaces that support psychological transitions between different activities and contexts.
- **Space for emergence:** Maintain some empty space—both physically and in your schedule—that allows for spontaneous authentic expression rather than constant predetermined activity.

This decluttering isn't about minimalist aesthetics but about creating environments where your authentic signals aren't lost in noise—where you can hear yourself think and feel without constant distraction.

SOCIAL ENVIRONMENT ASSESSMENT: THE PEOPLE FACTOR

It's easy to focus on the tangible—your workspace, your home—when considering what shapes your authenticity, but the invisible architecture of your relationships often holds far greater sway. While a cluttered desk might stifle creativity, a toxic relationship can erode your very sense of self. Your social environment, the people you surround yourself with, acts as a mirror, reflecting back not just who you are, but who you believe you should be. Thoughtful assessment of this landscape is crucial: are these relationships nurturing or draining? Do they encourage your growth or reinforce old, limiting patterns? Adjusting this landscape isn't about cutting people out, but about creating space for connections that honor your authentic self. It's about seeking out those who celebrate your vulnerability, challenge your growth, and provide a safe haven for your true expression. This intentional curation of your social surroundings creates the fertile ground where authenticity can take root and flourish, allowing you to live aligned with your values and purpose.

RELATIONSHIP INVENTORY: MAPPING YOUR SOCIAL TERRAIN

Understanding your current social environment provides the foundation for intentional shifts. Consider mapping your relationships along several important dimensions:

- **Authenticity support:** Which relationships encourage your genuine self-expression, and which require significant masking or performance?
- **Energy exchange:** Which connections consistently energize you, and which leave you drained?

- **Values alignment:** Where do you find easy agreement about what matters most, and where do you experience persistent value conflicts?
- **Growth orientation:** Which relationships support your development, and which seem invested in keeping you in familiar patterns?
- **Reciprocity balance:** Which connections feature mutual giving and receiving, and which feel consistently one-sided?

This inventory isn't about judging relationships as "good" or "bad" but about seeing clearly how different connections influence your authentic expression and where adjustments might be beneficial.

COMMUNITY SELECTION: FINDING YOUR AUTHENTICITY TRIBES

Beyond individual relationships, the communities you participate in create powerful contexts that either support or restrict authentic living:

- **Explicit value communities:** Groups organized around principles that matter to you naturally reinforce authentic expression aligned with those values.
- **Practice communities:** Circles focused on personal growth often explicitly value and support authentic expression.
- **Creative communities:** Groups engaged in artistic or innovative pursuits frequently create space for authentic voice and vision.
- **Service-oriented communities:** Environments focused on contributing to others often encourage genuine expression of compassion and purpose.
- **Learning communities:** Groups dedicated to growth and development typically value authentic questions and exploration.

These communities don't require abandoning existing connections but add key elements of support for aspects of your authentic self that may lack expression in other contexts.

CULTURAL CONTEXT NAVIGATION: AUTHENTICITY ACROSS ENVIRONMENTS

Different cultural contexts—whether ethnic, organizational, or social—have varying tolerance for and expressions of authenticity. Skillful navigation involves:

- **Cultural code-switching:** Developing the capacity to adjust your authentic expression to be receivable in different contexts without fundamental compromise.
- **Cultural value integration:** Finding ways to honor both your authentic values and the values of cultures important to your identity and belonging.

- **Expansion initiatives:** Gradually introducing more authentic expression in cultural contexts initially less receptive to it.
- **Selective engagement:** Making conscious choices about which cultural environments merit your full participation based on authenticity compatibility.
- **Community creation:** Sometimes fostering new micro-cultures that better support authentic living rather than trying to change established systems.

This navigation isn't about abandoning cultural identity but about finding the intersection between cultural belonging and authentic expression—a both/and rather than either/or approach.

Toxic Relationship Identification: Recognizing Fundamental Incompatibility

While most relationships can evolve to accommodate greater authenticity, some dynamics fundamentally depend on your inauthenticity and require more significant intervention:

Warning signs of toxic relationship patterns include:

- Consistent punishment of vulnerable authentic expression.
- Explicit demands to be someone you're not.
- Use of shame or rejection to control your behavior.
- Refusal to acknowledge or discuss relationship difficulties.
- Persistent undermining of your authentic goals and values.

These patterns differ from the normal adjustment challenges that occur when you become more authentic, representing instead fundamental opposition to your authentic expression.

> **"A toxic relationship keeps dragging you down. It never helps you in becoming better or growing as a person. You keep going back to pain and the sorrow keeps piling up."**

Responses to toxic dynamics might include:

- Clear boundary setting with consequences.
- Reduced investment and exposure.
- Professional support for navigation or transition.
- Termination of the relationship when necessary and possible.
- Compassionate understanding of the fears driving toxic behavior.

This assessment isn't about labeling people as toxic but about recognizing when relationship dynamics themselves fundamentally oppose authentic living, requiring more significant intervention than minor adjustments.

BUILDING A SUPPORT NETWORK: CREATING YOUR AUTHENTICITY ECOSYSTEM

Beyond addressing challenging relationships, proactively building a network that reinforces authentic living creates a powerful environmental support system:

- **Diversified support:** Different people who support different aspects of your authentic expression, rather than expecting any single relationship to meet all needs
- **Mutual growth connections:** Relationships where authentic living is a shared value and mutual encouragement
- **Accountability partnerships:** Specific relationships that include explicit agreements to support each other's alignment journey
- **Mentorship connections:** Relationships with those further along paths that matter to you who model integrated authentic living
- **Professional support:** Therapeutic or coaching relationships that provide specialized guidance for authenticity challenges

This network creates a social environment where authentic living becomes supported by your connections rather than constrained by them—where being your true self strengthens rather than threatens your sense of belonging.

These networks are not static; they evolve as you do, reflecting your changing needs and aspirations. They become a source of collective wisdom, offering diverse perspectives and practical guidance as you navigate the challenges of authentic living. It's about building a community that champions your growth, holds you accountable with compassion, and reminds you of your inherent worth, even when you doubt yourself. This network becomes a sanctuary, a place where you can recharge, reflect, and find the courage to continue your journey, knowing that you are not alone.

SCHEDULE AND TIME MANAGEMENT FOR AUTHENTICITY

Beyond physical and social environments, how you structure time significantly impacts your capacity for authentic living. Time management for authenticity differs from conventional productivity approaches, focusing on alignment rather than just efficiency.

Time Audit: Alignment Between Hours and Values

Begin by assessing how your current use of time reflects—or doesn't reflect—what truly matters to you:

- **Activity tracking:** For a typical week, record how you actually spend your time (not how you think or wish you spend it).
- **Energy mapping:** Note which activities energize you and which deplete you.
- **Values comparison:** Compare your time allocation with your stated values and priorities.
- **Obligation assessment:** Identify which time commitments feel authentically chosen versus externally imposed.
- **Flow evaluation:** Notice when you experience the engagement and timelessness associated with authentic absorption.

This audit often reveals surprising disconnects between stated values and actual time investment, creating clarity about potential adjustments that would better support authentic living.

Boundary-Based Scheduling: Protecting What Matters

Rather than filling every available moment, boundary-based scheduling creates protected time containers for priorities that support your authentic self:

- **Non-negotiable blocks:** Designate specific times for activities central to your authentic wellbeing and expression.
- **Buffer zones:** Create transition spaces between activities rather than packing commitments back-to-back.
- **Renewal repositories:** Schedule regular time for activities that reconnect you with your authentic self.
- **Technological boundaries:** Establish clear times when devices and digital demands are set aside.
- **"No" time:** Maintain portions of your schedule intentionally left open to prevent automatic overcommitment.

This approach shifts from reactive time management (responding to whatever demands arise) to proactive alignment (ensuring time allocation reflects authentic priorities).

Transition Buffers: Space Between Activities

The spaces between activities often determine whether you carry authentic presence from one context to another or operate in disconnected compartments:

- **Conscious transitions:** Brief rituals that help you close one activity before beginning another
- **Decompression zones:** Longer buffers after particularly intense or inauthentic-requiring activities

- **Context shifts:** Physical or mental practices that support moving between different authentic expressions
- **Integration pauses:** Moments to absorb experiences before moving to the next activity
- **Boundary reinforcement:** Clear markers between work, home, and other contexts that require different aspects of authentic expression

These buffers prevent the overflow of energy and attention from one context to another, supporting more integrated authentic presence across different life domains.

REDUCING OVERWHELM: SPACE FOR AUTHENTIC PRESENCE

Chronic busyness creates one of the most common barriers to authentic living—the sense that there's simply no time to check in with yourself in the thick of constant demands:

- **Commitment inventory:** Regularly assess which activities truly merit your time and which can be released
- **Perfectionism reduction:** Identify areas where "good enough" truly is sufficient, preserving energy for what matters most
- **Assistance activation:** Determine where help would create space for more authentic focus
- **Decision simplification:** Create systems that reduce repeated decision-making in non-essential areas
- **Expectation management:** Align commitments with realistic capacity rather than idealized productivity

This overwhelm reduction isn't about doing less for its own sake but about creating the spaciousness required for authentic presence rather than constant reactive doing.

RHYTHMS VERSUS ROUTINES: FLEXIBLE STRUCTURES FOR AUTHENTICITY

While conventional productivity often emphasizes set routines, authentic living typically benefits from more flexible rhythms that honor changing needs:

- **Core practices with flexible timing:** Maintaining consistent what with adaptable when.
- **Season-appropriate adjustments:** Adapting time structures to different life phases and external conditions.
- **Energy-based scheduling:** Aligning activities with your natural energy patterns rather than arbitrary clock divisions.
- **Intuition balancing structure:** Creating enough consistency for stability while allowing space for authentic responsiveness.
- **Progress not perfection:** Viewing time management as an ongoing experiment rather than a fixed system to perfect.

These rhythmic approaches support authentic living by creating helpful structure without tough constraints that override your genuine needs and natural cycles.

Media and Information Diet: Feeding Your Authentic Self

Just as physical nutrition affects bodily health, your information consumption greatly influences your emotional wellbeing and capacity for authentic presence. What you regularly read, watch, listen to, and otherwise take in shapes your internal landscape.

Consumption Awareness: The Invisible Influence

Begin by simply noticing how different types of information inputs affect your emotional state and authentic connection:

- **Baseline influence:** How does your current media diet affect your overall mood, energy, and thought patterns?
- **Immediate impacts:** What shifts do you notice in your state immediately after consuming different types of content?
- **Lingering effects:** Which information sources leave persistent impacts hours or days after consumption?
- **Comparison triggers:** What inputs consistently stimulate unhelpful comparison or inadequacy?
- **Authenticity resonance:** Which sources seem to reinforce your connection to your true self versus disconnecting you from it?

This awareness often reveals surprising patterns about how seemingly neutral or positive inputs might actually undermine your authentic presence and emotional wellbeing.

Intentional Intake: Curating Your Information Inputs

Building on this awareness, you can make more conscious choices about what you allow into your mental and emotional space:

- **Value alignment:** Selecting information sources that reinforce rather than contradict your authentic values
- **Inspiration versus depletion:** Choosing inputs that energize rather than exhaust your capacity for authentic living
- **Truth versus distortion:** Developing discernment about sources that offer genuine perspective versus manipulation

- **Growth orientation:** Favoring content that expands your understanding versus reinforcing existing biases or fears
- **Diversity with boundaries:** Exposing yourself to varied perspectives while maintaining limits around toxic or depleting content

This curation isn't about avoiding challenging information but about ensuring your overall information diet supports rather than undermines your capacity for authentic presence.

DIGITAL BOUNDARIES: TECHNOLOGICAL SELF-PROTECTION

Given the overwhelming volume of available information and the algorithms designed to maximize engagement rather than wellbeing, specific digital boundaries become essential:

- **Consumption timing:** Designating specific times for information intake rather than constant accessibility
- **Notification management:** Limiting alerts to truly time-sensitive matters rather than constant interruption
- **Platform limitations:** Restricting or eliminating platforms that consistently trigger comparison, inadequacy, or anxiety
- **Quantity constraints:** Setting concrete limits on consumption of potentially depleting content (news, social media, etc.)
- **Tech-free zones:** Creating physical spaces and time periods completely free from digital intrusion

These boundaries protect your limited attention—perhaps your most precious resource for authentic living—from being constantly hijacked by external inputs designed to capture rather than serve you.

INSPIRATION CURATION: SURROUNDING YOURSELF WITH WHAT MATTERS

Beyond limiting depleting inputs, actively cultivating sources of authentic inspiration creates an information environment that regularly reconnects you with what matters most:

- **Wisdom traditions:** Texts and teachings that have stood the test of time in supporting human flourishing
- **Artistic nourishment:** Creative works that awaken your capacity for beauty, meaning, and authentic expression
- **Nature connection:** Regular exposure to the profound perspective and sensory presence natural settings provide
- **Authentic voices:** Contemporary sources that speak truth with integrity rather than chasing engagement metrics
- **Personal anchors:** Maintaining collections of quotes, images, stories, or other content that reliably reconnects you with your authentic priorities

This intentional curation creates an environment where your authentic values and priorities are regularly reinforced rather than constantly undermined by misaligned inputs.

Mindful Media Engagement: Conscious Consumption

Even with carefully selected information sources, how you engage with content significantly affects its impact on your authentic presence:

- **Active versus passive consumption:** Bringing critical thinking and personal reflection to information intake rather than absorptive consumption
- **Intentional purpose:** Clarifying why you're engaging with particular content—education, entertainment, connection, escape—and whether it's serving that purpose
- **Bodily awareness:** Maintaining connection to physical sensations while consuming information, noticing tension, shallow breathing, or other signs of impact
- **Conscious transitions:** Creating clear beginnings and endings to media consumption rather than ambient background exposure
- **Reflective integration:** Taking time to consider how information connects to your authentic values and experience rather than simply moving to the next input

This mindful engagement transforms your relationship with information from passive consumption to active discernment, supporting integration with your authentic perspective rather than unconscious absorption of external viewpoints.

The Environmental Integration Process

The integration of the environmental process into authentic living isn't about isolating yourself in a curated bubble, but about recognizing the dynamic interplay between your inner and outer worlds. It's about consciously shaping your surroundings—both physical and social—to support your genuine expression. This means discerning which environments nourish your soul and which drain your energy, and then making intentional choices to align your external reality with your internal values. It's about creating spaces that reflect your authentic self, fostering relationships that celebrate your vulnerability, and navigating societal pressures with a grounded sense of integrity. By actively participating in the co-creation of your environment, you become a powerful force for authenticity, not just for yourself, but for those around you, cultivating a world where genuine connection and mindful living thrive.

It's a daily, intentional practice of conscious curation. Beyond the physical, it's about cultivating intentional social behaviors. This means setting clear boundaries in your interactions, choosing to engage in conversations that are meaningful and authentic, and limiting exposure to draining or toxic relationships. It involves practicing active listening, not just to others, but to your own inner voice, and prioritizing activities that align with your values and passions. It's about creating pockets of solitude for reflection and self-care, and consciously choosing to spend time with people who celebrate your authenticity. These daily, intentional behaviors, woven into the fabric of your life, gradually transform your environment into a sanctuary that supports and amplifies your truest self.

As you implement these environmental adjustments, remember that the goal isn't perfection but progress—creating conditions increasingly aligned with your authentic self. Start with the changes that seem most accessible and impactful for your particular situation rather than trying to transform everything at once.

Notice, too, the reciprocal relationship between inner and outer alignment. As you create more supportive environments, authentic expression becomes easier. As authentic expression increases, you'll naturally find yourself drawn to more supportive environments, creating a positive spiral of increasing alignment.

In the next section, we'll explore how to handle the resistance and setbacks that inevitably arise as you align your life more closely with your authentic self—both the internal resistance that emerges from habitual patterns and the external pushback that often accompanies significant change.

The Natural Challenges of Authentic Living

As you begin integrating authentic living practices into your daily life, you'll inevitably encounter both internal resistance and external pushback. This resistance isn't a sign of failure or an indication that something is wrong with your approach. Rather, it's a natural and predictable part of any significant change process.

Understanding common patterns of resistance and developing specific strategies for navigating them transforms these challenges from discouraging obstacles into anticipated aspects of the journey. With this preparation, you can meet resistance with curiosity and skill rather than surprise and defeat.

Internal Resistance Patterns

Some of the most powerful resistance to authentic living comes from within—parts of yourself that, for various reasons, find the shift toward greater authenticity threatening or uncomfortable.

The Comfort of Familiarity: Why We Resist Positive Change

One of the most puzzling aspects of personal growth is why we sometimes cling to patterns that cause suffering rather than embracing healthier alternatives. This resistance often stems from the powerful pull of the familiar:

- **Predictability security:** Even painful patterns offer the comfort of knowing what to expect, while new ways of being introduce uncertainty.
- **Identity investment:** Long-standing patterns often become woven into your sense of self—changing them can feel like losing rather than liberating yourself.
- **Energy conservation:** Your brain naturally prefers established neural pathways, which require less energy than creating new ones, regardless of whether they lead to positive outcomes.
- **Secondary benefits:** Inauthentic patterns may provide indirect advantages (sympathy, lowered expectations, avoidance of challenging situations) that you're reluctant to surrender.
- **Developmental appropriateness:** Patterns that once served essential protective functions can be difficult to release even when they're no longer necessary.

Recognizing these natural tendencies toward the familiar helps normalize the internal resistance that arises during authentic living efforts. This resistance doesn't mean you don't want to change—it means you're human, with a brain and nervous system designed to conserve energy and maintain stability.

Fear Responses to Authentic Living: The Anxiety of Change

Specific fears commonly emerge as you move toward greater authenticity, triggering protective responses that can derail your efforts if not recognized and addressed:

- **Rejection fear:** Concern that authentic expression will lead to social exclusion or abandonment.
- **Identity fear:** Worry about who you'll be if you release familiar masks and patterns.
- **Success fear:** Anxiety about the responsibility that might come with living more authentically.
- **Visibility fear:** Discomfort with being truly seen rather than hiding behind performance.
- **Capability fear:** Doubt about your ability to navigate life from authentic presence rather than conditioned strategies.

These fears typically manifest as physical tension, procrastination, sudden doubt about your path, or a compelling urge to return to familiar patterns. Recognizing them as fear responses rather than rational objections helps you engage with them appropriately—with compassion and understanding rather than either suppression or uncritical acceptance.

Inner Critic Activation: The Judge Awakens

As you practice more authentic living, your inner critic—that internalized voice of judgment and evaluation—often becomes more active rather than less, at least initially. This increased criticism typically includes:

- **Authenticity questioning:** "Who do you think you are to claim this as your authentic self?"
- **Progress minimization:** "After all this work, you're still reacting the same old way."

- **Perfectionist demands:** "If you were really committed to authentic living, you'd never fall back into these patterns."
- **Comparative judgment:** "Look how much more authentic/evolved/aware others are."
- **Future catastrophizing:** "If you continue being this authentic, you'll end up alone/broke/rejected."

This heightened inner criticism doesn't indicate failure but actually signals that meaningful change is occurring—your internal system is noticing the shifts and attempting to protect you by encouraging return to familiar territory. Recognizing this pattern allows you to work with critical thoughts rather than being hijacked by them.

Identity Protection Mechanisms: Preserving the Status Quo

At a deeper level, significant resistance often emerges from parts of yourself invested in maintaining your current identity—even when that identity includes limitations and suffering:

- **Selective memory:** Forgetting the costs of old patterns while magnifying the challenges of new ones
- **Evidence filtering:** Noticing information that confirms the impossibility of change while dismissing signs of progress
- **Self-fulfilling prophecies:** Unconsciously creating situations that prove authentic living "doesn't work"
- **Moving goalposts:** Continually redefining what counts as "real" change to maintain the perception that you haven't achieved it
- **Identity drama:** Creating crises or conflicts that pull you back into familiar roles when authentic presence starts feeling too unfamiliar

These protection mechanisms operate largely outside conscious awareness, making them particularly effective at derailing authentic living efforts. Bringing them into awareness reduces their power, allowing you to recognize and navigate them when they arise.

Energy Conservation Instincts: The Efficiency Problem

Your system's natural tendency toward energy efficiency creates another subtle but powerful form of resistance:

- **Initial effort spike:** Authentic living initially requires more energy than automatic patterns, triggering conservation instincts
- **Fatigue vulnerability:** When tired or stressed, your capacity for the extra effort of authenticity naturally diminishes
- **Attentional limitations:** Maintaining awareness of authentic choices requires resources that deplete over time without renewal

- **Decision fatigue:** Each authentic choice draws from a limited daily reserve of decision-making energy
- **Habit gravity:** The pull of established neural pathways strengthens with stress, tiredness, or overwhelm

This energy-related resistance explains why authentic living often feels easier during low-stress periods and more challenging during demanding times. Recognizing this pattern helps you adjust expectations and support accordingly rather than interpreting temporary returns to old patterns as fundamental failures.

External Pushback and Relationship Dynamics

Beyond internal resistance, authentic living frequently triggers pushback from your social environment. Understanding these external dynamics helps you navigate them skillfully rather than being surprised or derailed by them.

System Homeostasis: The Status Quo Defense

Any system—whether a family, workplace, or friendship circle—naturally resists change in its established patterns, regardless of whether those patterns are healthy. This resistance isn't personal but systemic:

- **Role reinforcement:** Others unconsciously encouraging you to maintain familiar roles that stabilize the system.
- **Change dampening:** Small adjustments in others' behavior that counteract your moves toward authenticity.
- **Symptom redistribution:** When you stop carrying certain emotions or responsibilities, they often shift to others in the system.
- **Escalation sequences:** Patterns of interaction that intensify when you deviate from expected responses.
- **Predicted outcome emphasis:** Others highlighting potential negative consequences of your authentic choices.

This systemic resistance occurs even in generally supportive relationships, as all systems naturally work to maintain their established equilibrium. Recognizing this helps you respond to pushback as a natural dynamic rather than deliberate opposition.

The status quo defense, that insidious resistance to change, isn't just about clinging to comfort; it's a subtle act of self-preservation, a primal instinct to protect the familiar, even when it's detrimental. It whispers insidious lies, painting change as a threat to your very identity, masking fear as practicality. Recognizing this defense is crucial, for it often operates unconsciously, subtly sabotaging your growth and authenticity. It's about questioning the "shoulds" and "always haves" that bind you, acknowledging that the familiar can be a cage as much as a comfort. By confronting this resistance with courage and curiosity, you unlock the potential for profound transformation, allowing your authentic self to break free from the limitations of the past and embrace the possibilities of the future.

DIRECT OPPOSITION: WHEN OTHERS ACTIVELY RESIST

In some cases, particularly when your authentic choices threaten others' comfort or control, you may encounter more active and deliberate resistance:

- **Critical commentary:** Direct criticism of your authentic expressions or choices.
- **Pathologizing language:** Framing your changes as problems, issues, or concerning developments.
- **Historical reminders:** References to past failures or vulnerabilities to undermine confidence.
- **Either/or ultimatums:** Presenting choices between authenticity and relationship continuation.
- **Emotional leverage:** Using guilt, fear, or obligation to pressure return to previous patterns.

This direct opposition often emerges from others' genuine fear rather than malice—fear of what your changes might mean for them or for a relationship they value. Understanding this fear-based motivation helps you respond with compassion rather than defensiveness, even while maintaining your authentic boundaries.

INDIRECT UNDERMINING: THE SUBTLE SABOTAGE

Not all external resistance is direct. Often the most effective opposition comes through subtle, sometimes unconscious undermining:

- **Selective attention:** Noticing and commenting when you fall short of authenticity while ignoring progress.
- **Convenient forgetting:** "Forgetting" agreements that support your authentic choices.
- **Mixed messages:** Verbal support coupled with nonverbal disapproval or contradiction.
- **Help that hinders:** Assistance offered in ways that actually make authentic choices more difficult.
- **Space invasion:** Gradually encroaching on time or resources you've designated for authentic living.

These indirect forms of sabotage can be particularly challenging to address because they're often plausibly deniable—the person may not even be conscious of how their behavior undermines your efforts. Clear, specific feedback about the impact of these behaviors, delivered with compassion, creates the best opportunity for change.

ROLE REINFORCEMENT: THE PULL OF OTHERS' EXPECTATIONS

Relationships naturally develop expectations about who you are and how you'll behave. When you begin showing up differently, others often work to pull you back into familiar roles:

- **Identity reminders:** "You've always been the one who..."
- **Selective reinforcement:** Extra positive responses when you fulfill old roles, withdrawal when you don't.
- **Discomfort with new behaviors:** Subtle or overt signals that your authentic expressions are unwelcome.
- **Old story repetition:** Continually referencing past versions of you rather than acknowledging current reality.
- **Credit withholding:** Attributing positive changes to external factors rather than your authentic growth.

This role reinforcement often comes from a genuine place of confusion rather than manipulation—others are attempting to reconcile the person they've known with the more authentic person emerging. Patience with this adjustment process, combined with gentle persistence in your authentic expression, typically works better than confrontation.

Cultural and Community Pressure: The Broader Context

Beyond individual relationships, broader social contexts often exert pressure against authentic choices that deviate from community norms:

- **Success definitions:** Narrow cultural ideas about what constitutes a worthwhile life.
- **Gender expectations:** Powerful messaging about appropriate expression based on gender identity.
- **Religious frameworks:** Community standards about acceptable beliefs, values, and behaviors.
- **Family legacies:** Multigenerational patterns presented as immutable realities.
- **Professional cultures:** Field-specific norms that may conflict with authentic expression.

These broader pressures often operate as "the water you swim in"—so pervasive and normalized that they're difficult to even recognize, let alone challenge. Identifying them explicitly helps you discern which cultural norms align with your authentic values and which represent external conditioning you're ready to release.

SETBACK RECOVERY STRATEGIES

Despite your best intentions and efforts, you'll inevitably experience setbacks in your authentic living journey—moments where you return to old patterns or face challenges that temporarily derail your alignment. How you respond to these setbacks often determines whether they become valuable learning opportunities or discouraging dead ends.

Compassionate Self-Assessment: Evaluation Without Shame

The foundation for effective setback recovery is the ability to honestly assess what happened without spiraling into shame or self-criticism:

- **Fact-based observation:** Noting what actually occurred without exaggeration or minimization.
- **Pattern recognition:** Identifying whether this setback represents a familiar challenge or a new situation.
- **Trigger identification:** Recognizing specific circumstances that preceded the misalignment.
- **Needs assessment:** Understanding what legitimate needs you were trying to meet, even if the strategy wasn't optimal.
- **Strength acknowledgment:** Noticing what went well and where you showed resilience, even amidst difficulty.

This compassionate assessment creates the psychological safety necessary to learn from setbacks rather than becoming defensive or avoidant about them. It transforms setbacks from moral failings into data points that inform your continued growth.

Return Practices: Finding Your Way Back

Specific practices can help you return to authentic alignment after periods of disconnection:

- **Pattern interruption:** Simple actions that break the momentum of inauthentic patterns (deep breaths, physical movement, environment changes).
- **Reconnection rituals:** Brief practices that restore awareness of your authentic self and values.
- **Minimal restart:** The smallest possible authentic action that reestablishes alignment momentum.
- **Support activation:** Reaching out to understanding others who can help you regain perspective.
- **Sensory grounding:** Using physical sensations to return to present-moment awareness where authentic choice becomes possible.

These return practices reduce the common tendency for minor setbacks to expand into extended periods of misalignment. They operate like course corrections in navigation—small adjustments that prevent minor deviations from becoming major detours.

Learning Integration: Finding Value in Setbacks

Every setback contains valuable information when approached with curiosity rather than judgment:

- **Pattern clarification:** Each setback reveals more detail about specific triggers and vulnerabilities.
- **Needs identification:** Misalignments often point to legitimate needs seeking inadequate fulfillment.
- **Support assessment:** Setbacks highlight areas where additional resources or assistance would be helpful.
- **Strategy refinement:** Each challenge provides data for adjusting your authentic living approach.
- **Compassion expansion:** Working with your own setbacks develops greater understanding for others' struggles.

This learning orientation transforms setbacks from failures into essential feedback that makes your authentic living practice more robust and realistic. Without this feedback, authenticity remains an idealized concept rather than an embodied reality.

Support Activation: You Don't Have to Navigate Alone

Perhaps the most common mistake in setback recovery is attempting to handle everything independently, when connection often provides essential perspective and encouragement:

- **Accountability partnerships:** Relationships with explicit agreements about supporting each other's authentic living
- **Professional guidance:** Therapeutic or coaching support for navigating complex challenges
- **Community connection:** Groups where authentic struggles are normalized and supported
- **Structured programs:** Established approaches that provide frameworks for sustainable change
- **Inspirational resources:** Stories, teachings, or practices that reconnect you with authentic motivation

This support activation isn't a sign of weakness but of wisdom—recognizing that authentic living flourishes in connection rather than isolation, particularly during challenging periods.

Pattern Recognition: Your Personal Map

Over time, tracking your setbacks reveals personalized patterns that allow increasingly refined navigation:

- **Common triggers:** Specific situations, relationships, or internal states that reliably challenge your authenticity
- **Early warning signs:** Subtle indicators that misalignment is beginning before full disconnection occurs
- **Effective interventions:** Particular approaches that consistently help you return to alignment
- **Vulnerability cycles:** Predictable patterns in how setbacks tend to unfold for you specifically
- **Growth edges:** Areas where authentic living remains particularly challenging, indicating opportunities for focused attention

Imagine you're charting a course through uncharted territory – that's what recognizing your personal patterns is like. You're not just stumbling through; you're creating a detailed map of your inner world. Those "setbacks" become landmarks, revealing the triggers that derail you, the subtle whispers of misalignment, and the pathways that lead you back to yourself. You're no longer relying on a generic guidebook; you're becoming fluent in your own emotional language.

This personalized map transforms abstract concepts into tangible tools. It's about becoming an expert on your experience. You learn to predict your vulnerability cycles, pinpoint your growth edges, and develop interventions that resonate with your unique rhythm. Each trigger you identify, each early warning sign you recognize, each vulnerability cycle you understand, strengthens your ability to navigate the complexities of authentic living. It's a shift from following someone else's directions to trusting your own inner compass. This isn't just about learning authenticity; it's about embodying it, transforming knowledge into wisdom.

Pattern recognition changes generic authentic living practices into a customized approach tailored to your specific challenges and strengths. It represents the evolution from following external guidance to developing your own embodied wisdom.

> "The compass of your life is your heart. Your true north is the direction it points when nothing else is around." - Prem Rawat

THE PROGRESS PARADOX

Perhaps the most confusing aspect of authentic living involves the non-linear, sometimes contradictory nature of growth in this area. Understanding these paradoxical patterns prevents discouragement when progress doesn't follow expected trajectories.

NON-LINEAR DEVELOPMENT: THE SPIRAL PATH

Authentic living rarely develops in a straight line of continuous improvement. Instead, it typically follows a spiral pattern with several key characteristics:

- **Revisiting territory:** Returning to similar challenges at deeper levels rather than encountering completely new territory.
- **Integration cycles:** Periods of active growth followed by necessary consolidation phases.
- **Apparent regression:** Temporary returns to old patterns that actually facilitate deeper learning.
- **Quantum shifts:** Sudden breakthroughs after periods of seeming stagnation.
- **Simultaneous growth and challenge:** Increasing capacity alongside increasing awareness of limitations.

This spiral nature explains why authentic living often feels like you're covering familiar ground—you are, but with greater awareness and capacity each time, gradually transforming your relationship with core challenges rather than bypassing them entirely.

Apparent Regression: When Backward Means Forward

Some of the most confusing moments in authentic living occur when you seem to lose ground, returning to patterns you thought you'd moved beyond. Often these apparent regressions actually facilitate deeper growth:

- **Excavation opportunities:** Old patterns resurfacing to be addressed more thoroughly.
- **Integration necessities:** Temporary returns that allow consolidation of new awareness.
- **Authenticity expansions:** Accessing aspects of yourself previously excluded from "acceptable" identity.
- **Stress testing:** Challenging circumstances revealing where authentic living needs strengthening.
- **Depth over performance:** Genuine development replacing superficial behavior change.

These regressions feel discouraging when judged by linear standards but make perfect sense within a more accurate understanding of how authentic integration actually occurs—through cycles of emergence, challenge, and incorporation rather than continuous forward progress.

Success Challenges: When Achievement Triggers Setbacks

Counterintuitively, periods of successful authentic living often trigger setbacks, creating confusion and discouragement if not understood as a natural pattern:

- **Identity stretching:** Success requires expansion beyond familiar self-concepts.
- **Visibility discomfort:** Achievement creating greater exposure than you're accustomed to handling.
- **Unconscious limits:** Success activating internal beliefs about what you deserve or are allowed to experience.
- **System adjustments:** Relationship dynamics shifting in response to your authentic achievements.
- **Balance recalibration:** New expressions requiring integration with existing aspects of life.

Recognizing these success-triggered challenges helps you anticipate and prepare for them rather than being blindsided when achievement is followed by unexpected difficulty maintaining authentic alignment.

The Myth of Arrival: Practice Not Perfection

One of the most persistent and unhelpful beliefs about authentic living is the idea that it's a destination you'll eventually reach completely—a state of perfect alignment you can achieve and maintain:

- **Completion fantasy:** The belief that authentic living will eventually become effortless and constant.
- **Binary thinking:** Viewing yourself as either "being authentic" or "not being authentic" rather than recognizing degrees of alignment.
- **Perfectionistic standards:** Judging normal fluctuations as failures rather than natural rhythms.
- **End-state orientation:** Focusing on achieving authentication" rather than engaging in ongoing practice.
- **Comparison distortion:** Measuring your authentic living journey against idealized images of others.

Releasing this myth of arrival transforms authentic living from an impossible standard to an ongoing practice—something you do rather than something you achieve once and for all. This shift dramatically reduces discouragement while supporting sustained engagement with the process.

Sustainable Pace Finding: The Marathon Not Sprint

The final paradox involves timing and sustainability—authentic living develops most effectively through consistent, moderate effort rather than intense bursts followed by exhaustion:

- **Minimum effective dose:** Finding the smallest regular practices that maintain alignment momentum.
- **Rest as productive:** Recognizing that integration periods are as essential as active growth phases.
- **Rhythm development:** Creating sustainable cycles of engagement, rest, and reflection.
- **Long-view perspective:** Measuring progress over months and years rather than days or weeks.
- **Life integration:** Weaving authentic living into your existing reality rather than treating it as a separate project.

This sustainable approach prevents the common pattern of enthusiastic beginning, burnout, abandonment, and renewed effort—the cycle that keeps authentic living perpetually in the "starting over" phase rather than deepening through consistent practice.

Working With Rather Than Against Resistance

As you encounter both internal resistance and external pushback, remember that the goal isn't to eliminate these natural responses but to work with them skillfully. Resistance itself isn't the problem—it's how you relate to resistance that determines whether it becomes an insurmountable obstacle or a valuable part of your growth process.

With this understanding of common resistance patterns and setback recovery strategies, you're better equipped to navigate the inevitable challenges of integrating authentic living into your daily reality. In the next section, we'll explore how to build relationships that honor your true self—creating connections that support rather than undermine your continuing journey toward emotional alignment.

Building Relationships That Honor Your True Self

While authentic living begins as an internal journey, it inevitably affects and is affected by your relationships. The people in your life can either powerfully support your authentic expression or consistently undermine it. Creating a relational environment that honors your true self becomes essential for sustainable authentic living.

This relational dimension involves both modifying existing connections and cultivating new relationships aligned with your authentic values. It requires recognizing that authenticity doesn't mean identical expression in all relationships, but rather finding ways to genuinely be yourself within different contexts and connections.

Authenticity in Existing Relationships

Most of us begin our authentic living journey already embedded in a network of relationships—family connections, friendships, romantic partnerships, professional associations—that formed under previous patterns of interaction. Navigating authenticity within these established relationships presents both challenges and opportunities.

Relationship Evolution: Natural Growth and Change

As you become more authentic, your relationships naturally change in response—sometimes gradually, sometimes dramatically. Understanding common evolutionary patterns helps you navigate this transition:

- **Initial disruption:** Short-term turbulence as established interaction patterns shift.
- **Renegotiation phase:** Period of adjusting expectations and finding new ways of relating.
- **Depth or distance:** Some relationships deepening through greater authenticity while others may become more limited.
- **Selective authenticity development:** Different aspects of your authentic self finding expression in different relationships.
- **Integration period:** Eventually establishing new relational equilibrium that accommodates your authentic expression.

This evolution doesn't necessarily mean losing connections, but it does typically involve transformation—relationships either grow to accommodate your authentic self or naturally shift to more peripheral positions in your life. This process happens with or without conscious intention, but awareness allows you to influence its direction.

"Evolution is a process of continuous branching and diversification from common trunks. This pattern of irreversible separation gives life's history its basic directionality." - Stephen Jay Gould.

COMMUNICATION APPROACHES: EXPRESSING AUTHENTIC NEEDS

How you communicate about your changing needs and expressions significantly impacts whether existing relationships can successfully evolve:

- **"I" language:** Framing changes in terms of your experience and needs rather than others' deficiencies.
- **Timing sensitivity:** Choosing moments for important conversations when both you and others have sufficient capacity.
- **Appreciation balance:** Acknowledging what works in the relationship alongside what you'd like to shift.
- **Curiosity cultivation:** Exploring others' experiences of the relationship with genuine interest.
- **Specific requests:** Clearly expressing what would support your authentic expression.

These communication approaches create opportunities for mutual understanding rather than defensive reactions. They recognize that authentic expression includes both honesty about your needs and care for the relationship itself.

Expressing authentic needs isn't about demanding or manipulating; it's about courageous self-disclosure, a practice of revealing your vulnerabilities and desires with clarity and respect. 1 It's a progressive journey, starting with internal awareness: recognizing what you truly require for your well-being. This then translates into assertive, not aggressive, communication, where you articulate your needs without compromising the needs of others. 2 It's an enlightening process, as you discover that expressing your needs doesn't diminish you; it actually empowers you and strengthens your relationships. By consistently practicing this, you educate others on how to treat you, fostering environments of mutual respect and understanding, and ultimately, paving the way for more genuine and fulfilling connections.

One client found a simple but powerful way to introduce authenticity into a long-standing friendship: "I realize I've been holding back parts of myself because I was afraid they might be too much for our friendship. I value our connection too much to keep pretending, though. Would you be open to me sharing more of what I'm really experiencing these days?"

Navigation of Resistance: Working with Others' Discomfort

Even with skillful communication, you'll likely encounter resistance as relationships adjust to your authentic expression. Productive responses to this resistance include:

- **Validation without agreement:** Acknowledging others' discomfort without abandoning your authentic needs.
- **Patience with adjustment:** Recognizing that adaptation takes time, especially in long-standing relationships.
- **Clear boundaries:** Maintaining limits around behavior you'll accept while allowing emotional reactions.
- **Underlying needs identification:** Looking for the legitimate concerns beneath surface resistance.
- **Mutual benefit emphasis:** Highlighting how authentic relationships serve everyone involved.

This navigation requires balancing compassion for others' adjustment process with commitment to your authentic expression. It avoids both rigid insistence on immediate acceptance and abandonment of authenticity to maintain relationship harmony.

Role Renegotiation: Shifting Longstanding Patterns

Many relationships assign implicit roles that become restrictive over time—the responsible one, the peacemaker, the organizer, the supporter. Authentic living often requires renegotiating these roles:

- **Pattern identification:** Naming long-established roles that no longer fit your authentic self.
- **Gradual adjustment:** Introducing changes incrementally rather than abruptly abandoning expected functions.
- **Reciprocity conversations:** Discussing how responsibilities and roles might be more equitably distributed.
- **Skill development support:** Helping others build capacity in areas you've traditionally managed.
- **Identity expansion:** Creating space in the relationship for previously unexpressed aspects of yourself.

This renegotiation acknowledges that established roles usually served important functions, addressing those needs while creating more flexibility and authenticity in how they're met. The goal isn't eliminating all roles but ensuring they remain freely chosen expressions rather than confining expectations.

Acceptance of Limitations: Recognizing Relationship Realities

Some relationships have inherent limitations in how much authenticity they can accommodate, due to their nature, history, or the other person's capacity. Wisdom involves recognizing these limitations without abandoning the connection entirely:

- **Context-appropriate authenticity:** Adjusting expectations based on the relationship's purpose and parameters.
- **Conscious choices:** Deciding which aspects of authenticity matter most in specific relationships.
- **Energy investment alignment:** Matching your emotional investment to a relationship's capacity for authentic connection.
- **Appreciation for what is:** Finding value in what a relationship does offer while acknowledging its limitations.
- **Supplemental connection:** Building additional relationships that support aspects of authenticity not accommodated in limited connections.

This acceptance isn't resignation but realism—recognizing that no single relationship can meet all authentic expression needs and that different connections serve different purposes in a full life. It allows you to maintain valuable but limited relationships without expecting them to accommodate your entire authentic self.

Attracting and Developing Authentic New Connections

It's not just about tweaking the relationships you already have; true authentic living often invites the creation of fresh connections, relationships born from your genuine expression. These aren't just surface-level acquaintances; they're the kind of bonds that resonate on a deeper level, built on shared values and mutual understanding. Because they begin with you showing up as your true self, there's a natural ease and depth to them, a sense of "finally, I'm seen." These connections aren't forced or contrived; they flow organically, like finding your tribe. You'll often find these relationships are less about playing roles and more about shared experiences, mutual support, and genuine connection. They become a safe haven, a space where you can be yourself without reservation, and where you're celebrated for your authenticity, not in spite of it. This allows you to build a supportive network that further strengthens your ability to live authentically in all areas of your life.

Authenticity as a Filter: Natural Selection Process

One of the most powerful aspects of authentic living is how it naturally attracts compatible connections while creating distance from incompatible ones:

- **Value visibility:** When you live your values openly, you become visible to others who share them.
- **Resonance recognition:** Authentic expression creates natural resonance with compatible people.
- **Efficiency effect:** Less time spent in superficial connections creates space for meaningful ones.
- **Mutual attraction patterns:** Others living authentically tend to recognize and appreciate your authentic expression.
- **Energy alignment:** Your genuine enthusiasm draws those interested in what truly matters to you.

This filtering effect operates without deliberate effort—simply expressing your authentic self creates a natural sorting process that brings compatible connections toward you while allowing incompatible ones to naturally fade. As one client observed, "I stopped working so hard to find 'my people' when I realized that being genuinely myself was the most effective way to become visible to them."

EARLY DISCLOSURE STRATEGIES: SETTING AUTHENTIC TONE

How you show up in the early stages of new relationships significantly influences whether they develop as authentic connections:

- **Appropriate vulnerability pacing:** Sharing authentic aspects of yourself at a rate that allows trust to develop naturally.
- **Values visibility:** Finding natural ways to indicate what matters most to you.
- **Boundary clarity:** Establishing clear limits that protect your authentic needs from the beginning.
- **Genuine curiosity:** Showing real interest in others' authentic experience rather than social performance.
- **Consistency practice:** Maintaining authentic expression across different interactions rather than dramatically shifting personas.

These approaches establish authenticity as a foundational expectation in the relationship from its earliest stages, creating a container where genuine connection can flourish without later requiring major adjustments or revelations.

RED FLAG RECOGNITION: IDENTIFYING AUTHENTICITY OBSTACLES

Not all new connections have potential for supporting authentic expression. Recognizing warning signs early prevents investment in relationships fundamentally at odds with your authentic self:

- **Persistent discomfort:** Consistent physical tension or unease in someone's presence.
- **Value minimization:** Dismissal or mockery of what matters most to you.
- **Authenticity interruption:** Changing subjects when conversation moves toward meaningful topics.
- **One-way disclosure patterns:** Expecting you to share openly while revealing little themselves.
- **Inconsistency markers:** Significant disconnects between stated values and observed behavior.

These red flags don't necessarily indicate "bad people" but signal connections unlikely to support authentic expression. Recognizing them early allows you to adjust investment accordingly rather than trying to force compatible connections where fundamental alignment is missing.

Shared Values Exploration: Finding Common Ground

While differences can enhance relationships, certain core value alignments create essential foundations for authentic connection:

- **Authenticity valuation:** Shared appreciation for honest expression over social performance.
- **Growth orientation:** Common interest in development and learning.
- **Communication styles:** Compatible approaches to addressing difficulties and differences.
- **Responsibility concepts:** Aligned understanding of personal agency and accountability.
- **Integrity definitions:** Similar views on the importance of consistency between words and actions.

This value exploration isn't about finding identical perspectives but discovering sufficient common ground in foundational areas while maintaining appreciation for differences in others. It creates relationships where authentic expression feels natural rather than constantly requiring translation or defense.

Vulnerability Pacing: Building Authentic Depth

Authentic relationships develop through gradually increasing vulnerability, paced appropriately to the relationship's context and development:

- **Reciprocity awareness:** Matching vulnerability levels rather than consistently being much more or less open than others.
- **Purpose-appropriate sharing:** Aligning vulnerability with the relationship's nature and purpose.
- **Response testing:** Starting with smaller authentic disclosures to assess how they're received.
- **Progressive openness:** Gradually increasing depth as trust and understanding develop.
- **Context sensitivity:** Recognizing that different relationships support different aspects and degrees of vulnerability.

This paced approach prevents both superficial connection (from insufficient vulnerability) and overwhelmed connection (from too much vulnerability too quickly). It creates relationships that deepen naturally through gradual, mutual authentic disclosure rather than forced intimacy or permanent guardedness.

Authentic Leadership and Influence

Beyond personal relationships, authentic expression significantly impacts how you influence others in leadership and mentor roles—whether formal or informal. This authentic influence creates a compound effect far beyond your immediate connections.

Leading from Authenticity: Impact Beyond Personal Benefit

Authentic leadership isn't just personally satisfying—it creates profound effects on those you influence:

- **Truth permission:** Your authenticity implicitly authorizes others to be more genuine.
- **Trust foundation:** Consistent authenticity builds the trust essential for effective guidance.
- **Value demonstration:** Embodying principles rather than just advocating them.
- **Inspiration rather than pressure:** Modeling authentic living draws others naturally rather than pushing them.
- **Resilience example:** Showing how authenticity supports navigation of real challenges.

This authentic influence operates whether you hold formal leadership positions or simply show up authentically in your everyday interactions. It creates cultural change through embodiment rather than promotion, with effects that often extend far beyond your awareness.

Permission-Giving Effect: Creating Space for Others

One of the most powerful aspects of authentic expression is how it creates implicit permission for others to be more authentic:

- **Vulnerability normalization:** Your comfort with imperfection makes it safer for others to be human.
- **Emotion legitimization:** Authentic expression of feelings validates others' emotional experiences.
- **Boundary modeling:** Clear limits demonstrate that self-respect and connection can coexist.
- **Value prioritization:** Choices aligned with values show others that authentic living is possible.
- **Reality acknowledgment:** Honesty about challenges counters perfectionist pretense.

This permission-giving effect often works invisibly—people rarely say "your authenticity inspired mine," but the impact happens nonetheless. It's one of the most significant ways authentic living contributes beyond personal wellbeing to cultural transformation.

AUTHENTIC AUTHORITY: HUMAN LEADERSHIP

Many people struggle with reconciling leadership roles with authentic expression, fearing that showing humanity will undermine their authority. In reality, the opposite typically occurs:

- **Trust through transparency:** Appropriate acknowledgment of limitations builds credibility rather than diminishing it.
- **Connection with competence:** Combining genuine humanity with skilled performance creates the strongest leadership impact.
- **Inspiration through integration:** Demonstrating authentic living while maintaining effectiveness inspires more than perfection pretense.
- **Flexible strength:** Authentic leadership adapts to circumstances rather than applying rigid formulas.
- **Sustainable influence:** Leadership grounded in authentic presence creates lasting impact rather than temporary compliance.

This authentic authority doesn't mean sharing every thought or feeling in leadership contexts, but it does involve bringing genuine presence rather than performance to your influence roles. The authenticity is in the quality of presence, not necessarily in the quantity of disclosure.

VULNERABILITY WITHOUT OVERSHARING: APPROPRIATE OPENNESS

In leadership and influence positions, calibrating vulnerability appropriately becomes particularly important:

- **Purpose-driven disclosure:** Sharing that serves the context and others' needs rather than personal unburdening.
- **Processed vulnerability:** Revealing challenges you've integrated rather than raw emotional material.
- **Strength-based openness:** Vulnerability that demonstrates capability to handle difficulty rather than seeking rescue.
- **Boundary-conscious sharing:** Maintaining appropriate professional or role boundaries while being genuinely human.
- **Context sensitivity:** Adjusting vulnerability to the setting, relationship, and purpose.

This calibrated vulnerability creates connection without confusion, showing humanity while maintaining the containment appropriate to leadership roles. It demonstrates that authentic expression can enhance rather than undermine effectiveness in influence positions.

Values-Based Influence: Changing Culture Through Being

Perhaps the most profound impact of authentic living comes through its subtle influence on broader culture—shifting what's normal, expected, and valued in your environments:

- **Embodied alternatives:** Demonstrating different ways of being rather than just talking about them.
- **Quiet permission:** Creating space for others to express previously suppressed authentic aspects.
- **Cultural expansion:** Broadening what's considered acceptable and valuable in your contexts.
- **Stereotype disruption:** Challenging limiting assumptions through authentic expression that doesn't fit expected molds.
- **Integration modeling:** Showing how authentic living enhances rather than conflicts with effectiveness.

This values-based influence rarely happens through deliberate advocacy but through consistent embodiment of different possibilities. It's the difference between telling others that authentic expression matters and showing them its value through your lived example.

Navigating Different Relationship Types Authentically

Authentic expression looks different across various relationship contexts, each with its own opportunities and challenges for genuine presence.

Family Dynamics: Balancing History and Growth

Family relationships carry the longest history and often the strongest expectations, creating unique authenticity challenges:

- **Role evolution:** Finding ways to grow beyond childhood roles while maintaining connection.
- **Selective battles:** Choosing which aspects of authenticity matter most in family contexts.
- **Transgenerational awareness:** Recognizing how family patterns extend beyond individuals.
- **Boundary practice:** Often requiring clearer limits than other relationships due to established patterns.
- **Acceptance balance:** Finding peace with aspects unlikely to change while not abandoning authentic needs.

This navigation acknowledges both the deep importance of family connections and their sometimes limited capacity for supporting all aspects of authentic expression. It seeks the maximum authenticity possible within realistic understanding of established family systems.

WORKPLACE RELATIONSHIPS: PROFESSIONAL AUTHENTICITY

Work contexts have distinct parameters around authentic expression, requiring thoughtful navigation rather than either complete conformity or disregard for professional norms:

- **Values alignment:** Seeking roles and organizations with cultures compatible with your core values.
- **Appropriate vulnerability:** Finding the right balance of humanity and professionalism.
- **Contribution focus:** Expressing authenticity through quality work reflecting your genuine strengths.
- **Strategic authenticity:** Choosing which aspects of authentic self best serve the work context.
- **Initiative taking:** Creating space for authentic expression by introducing new approaches when possible.

This professional authenticity doesn't mean ignoring context-appropriate boundaries but finding ways to bring genuine presence and values alignment to your work identity rather than maintaining a completely separate "work self" disconnected from your authentic core.

FRIENDSHIP EVOLUTION: AUTHENTIC CONNECTION DIVERSITY

Friendships often provide the most flexible container for authentic expression, with different connections supporting different aspects of your authentic self:

- **Friendship portfolio approach:** Building various relationships that collectively support your full authentic expression.
- **Depth variation:** Maintaining both deep, vulnerable connections and more activity-based friendships.
- **Growth accompaniment:** Seeking friendships that encourage your continued authentic development.
- **Historical navigation:** Evolving long-term friendships to accommodate your authentic growth.
- **Community building:** Creating friend groups and social circles that value authentic expression.

This friendship evolution acknowledges that different connections serve different functions in a well-rounded social life. Rather than expecting every friendship to accommodate your entire authentic self, you create a network of relationships that collectively support full expression.

INTIMATE PARTNERSHIPS: THE AUTHENTICITY LABORATORY

Romantic partnerships typically involve the most comprehensive authentic expression, creating both the greatest challenges and opportunities for aligned living:

- **Selection fundamentals:** Choosing partners who demonstrate genuine interest in and capacity for authentic connection.
- **Growth commitment:** Building relationships that embrace ongoing authentic development for both people.
- **Vulnerability progression:** Gradually increasing authentic disclosure as trust and understanding develop.
- **Conflict as opportunity:** Using disagreements as gateways to deeper authentic understanding.
- **Balance maintenance:** Creating space for both individual authenticity and shared identity.

This partnership authenticity doesn't mean perfect alignment or constant deep sharing but rather creating a relationship container where authenticity is fundamental to the connection rather than threatening to it. It involves building a "we" that enhances rather than diminishes each individual's authentic expression.

PARENTING AND MENTORING: AUTHENTIC GUIDANCE

Relationships where you guide others' development present unique authenticity opportunities through modeling genuine presence while respecting autonomy:

- **Appropriate transparency:** Sharing personal experiences and challenges in ways that serve others' growth.
- **Values realization:** Demonstrating authentic living rather than just advocating it.
- **Authentic boundaries:** Showing how limits and authentic expression work together.
- **Growth modeling:** Letting others witness your continued development and learning.
- **Autonomy respect:** Supporting others' authentic paths even when different from yours.

This mentorship authenticity creates relationships where your genuine presence becomes a resource for others without imposing your specific authentic expression as the template they should follow. It offers authentic guidance while honoring each person's unique authentic development.

THE RELATIONSHIP ECOSYSTEM

Think of your life as a living, breathing ecosystem of relationships – a complex web of connections that shapes your well-being and influences your life. Authentic living and emotional intelligence become the vital nutrients that nourish this ecosystem, fostering healthy growth and resilience. When you prioritize genuine expression, you create an environment where trust and vulnerability can flourish. You cultivate relationships built on honesty, where boundaries are respected, and emotional needs are met. This, in turn, strengthens the entire ecosystem, creating a supportive network that empowers you to thrive.

As you create a relationship network that supports authentic living, remember that no single connection—no matter how important—can meet all your authentic expression needs. Just as a healthy ecosystem contains diverse elements that together create a thriving whole, your relationship ecosystem requires various connections that collectively support your full authentic self.

This diversity isn't a deficiency but a strength—different relationships naturally accommodate different aspects of authentic expression, creating a network that supports your whole self through complementary connections rather than placing impossible expectations on any single relationship.

In the next section, we'll explore how to sustain your emotional alignment journey over time—creating practices and approaches that support authentic living as an ongoing reality rather than a temporary project or distant ideal.

Sustaining Your Emotional Alignment Journey

The journey of authentic living isn't a short-term project or one-time transformation but an ongoing practice that unfolds throughout your life. While initial enthusiasm can carry you through early stages, sustainable authentic living requires approaches that work with rather than against your natural tendencies and life circumstances.

This sustainability isn't about perfection or unwavering consistency but about creating conditions where authentic living becomes your default orientation, with effective ways to return when you inevitably drift into old patterns. It's about turning authentic living from something you do occasionally into something you are consistently, even as the specific expression evolves over time.

Customizing Your Practice Toolkit

The practices that support authentic living aren't one-size-fits-all. What works beautifully for someone else might feel forced or ineffective for you. Creating a personalized approach aligned with your unique temperament, circumstances, and natural tendencies dramatically increases sustainability.

Personal Assessment: Finding Your Authentic Path

Begin by honestly assessing which aspects of authentic living come naturally to you and which require more deliberate attention:

- **Awareness strengths:** Do you naturally notice physical sensations, emotional shifts, thought patterns, or interpersonal dynamics?
- **Expression tendencies:** Are you more comfortable with verbal sharing, written reflection, creative expression, or embodied communication?
- **Connection patterns:** Do you process experiences internally first or through dialogue? In one-on-one conversations or group settings?
- **Energy management:** Are you energized by intensive immersion or gradual, steady engagement? By structure or flexibility?
- **Learning preferences:** Do you integrate new patterns better through intellectual understanding, emotional experience, physical practice, or practical application?

This assessment isn't about identifying deficiencies but about recognizing your natural tendencies so you can work with rather than against your authentic inclinations. When authentic living practices align with your natural style, they require less willpower and become more sustainable over time.

Temperament Considerations: Honoring Your Nature

Your basic temperament—the innate tendencies you've had since childhood—significantly influences which authentic living approaches will be most sustainable for you:

- **For analytical types:** Practices that engage your natural curiosity and love of understanding, like journaling with specific reflection questions or tracking patterns in your authentic expression
- **For emotional types:** Approaches that honor your natural feeling orientation, such as arts-based expression or emotionally connective sharing circles
- **For practical types:** Concrete, action-oriented practices that produce tangible results, like creating specific authentic living experiments with measurable outcomes
- **For contemplative types:** Reflective practices that allow space for deep consideration, such as meditation or extended time in nature
- **For social types:** Relationally-based approaches like buddy systems, group practices, or coaching relationships

These temperament-aligned approaches reduce the friction that occurs when you try to force yourself into authentic living practices that fundamentally conflict with how you're naturally wired. They transform practice from constant effort to natural extension of who you already are.

> **"A great part of what appears in life as luck is found on closer examination to be closely bound up with temperament." - Samuel Butler.**

Temperament, that unique blend of innate traits and tendencies, isn't a fixed destiny, but rather the raw material from which you sculpt your authentic self. Understanding it is like discovering the blueprint of your inner architecture. It reveals your natural strengths and vulnerabilities, guiding you towards environments and practices that resonate with your core. Don't see it as a limitation; see it as a compass. By acknowledging your temperament, you can navigate the world with greater self-awareness, cultivating resilience and crafting a life that honors your inherent nature, allowing your unique brilliance to shine.

Temperament is like the underlying melody of your being, the consistent rhythm that colors your responses and interactions. It's not the whole song, but it profoundly influences the harmony and tone.

LIFE STAGE FACTORS: RIGHT TIMING FOR YOU

Different life phases present distinct challenges and opportunities for authentic living, requiring adjustments to maintain sustainability:

- **High-demand periods:** During intensely busy phases (career establishment, young children, caregiving), emphasizing micro-practices and integration rather than time-intensive approaches.
- **Transition times:** During major life changes, focusing on foundational grounding practices that provide stability amid change.
- **Stability phases:** In relatively settled periods, potentially engaging in deeper, more transformative authentic living work.
- **Resource-limited times:** During illness, grief, or overwhelm, simplifying to the most essential supportive practices.
- **Expansion periods:** When circumstances allow, potentially exploring new dimensions of authentic expression.

This life-stage sensitivity prevents the discouragement that comes from trying to maintain practices misaligned with your current life realities. It acknowledges that authentic living looks different across life's varying seasons, with sustainability requiring adaptation rather than rigid consistency.

STRENGTH-BASED FOCUS: BUILDING ON YOUR FOUNDATION

Rather than approaching authentic living as fixing deficiencies, focusing on developing your existing strengths creates more sustainable momentum:

- **Natural capacities:** Identifying aspects of authentic living that already come relatively easily to you.
- **Interest alignment:** Connecting practices to topics and approaches you genuinely enjoy.
- **Success patterns:** Noticing what conditions have supported your authentic expression in the past.

- **Positive reinforcement:** Emphasizing progress and growth rather than focusing primarily on shortcomings.
- **Enjoyment factor:** Selecting approaches that contain elements of genuine pleasure and satisfaction.

This strength-based orientation transforms authentic living from dutiful self-improvement to energizing self-expression. It creates positive reinforcement cycles where each authentic step generates energy for the next rather than depleting limited willpower reserves.

Minimum Effective Practice: Less Can Be More

In authentic living, the simplest sustainable approach often proves more effective than elaborate practices that are difficult to maintain. Finding your minimum effective practice involves:

- **Simplicity focus:** Identifying the simplest interventions that create meaningful shifts in your authentic alignment.
- **Highest leverage points:** Determining which aspects of authentic living create the greatest ripple effects in your particular case.
- **Elimination of extras:** Removing unnecessary complications from your practice that don't contribute to core benefits.
- **Frequency over duration:** Often choosing brief, regular practices over longer, occasional ones.
- **Integration emphasis:** Looking for ways to enhance authenticity within existing activities rather than always adding new ones.

This minimum effective approach prevents the common cycle of enthusiastic over-commitment followed by abandonment when complex practices prove unsustainable. It creates a foundation of consistency that can expand organically as capacity develops.

For authentic living to become your default orientation rather than an occasional project, it must integrate into the fabric of your daily life rather than remaining a separate activity competing for limited time and attention.

Habit Stacking: Attachment to Existing Patterns

One of the most effective ways to establish sustainable authentic living practices is connecting them to habits you already maintain consistently:

- **Morning routines:** Attaching brief authentic check-ins to existing morning patterns like coffee preparation or showering.
- **Transition moments:** Using commutes, walking between meetings, or changing tasks as triggers for authentic reconnection.

- **Digital habits:** Connecting authenticity reminders to technology use, like a brief awareness practice before checking email.
- **Physical activities:** Incorporating authentic presence into regular exercise or movement.
- **Evening patterns:** Adding reflection or integration practices to existing bedtime routines.

This habit stacking dramatically reduces the effort required to maintain authentic living practices by using the momentum of established patterns rather than requiring brand new habit formation. The existing habit becomes the reliable trigger for authentic living elements.

Micro-Practices: Brief but Powerful Interventions

For busy lives, micro-practices—interventions requiring seconds or minutes rather than extended time—often prove most sustainable:

- **Three conscious breaths:** Brief but complete awareness of three breath cycles.
- **Body scan light:** Quick head-to-toe awareness of physical sensations.
- **Value touchstone:** Momentary reconnection with a core value or intention.
- **Authentic check:** Brief internal inquiry about what you're genuinely feeling or needing.
- **Presence reset:** Short sensory grounding in your immediate environment.

These micro-practices don't require scheduling or special conditions but can be inserted into natural pauses throughout your day. Their brevity makes them accessible even during busy periods, maintaining continuity in your authentic living practice when longer approaches might be temporarily impossible.

Trigger-Based Reminders: Environmental Cues

Using specific environmental cues as prompts for authentic reconnection creates automatic rather than willpower-dependent practice:

- **Visual triggers:** Objects or images strategically placed in your environment that remind you of authentic priorities.
- **Digital notifications:** Carefully selected alerts or reminders that prompt authentic check-ins.
- **Routine activities:** Using regular actions like hand-washing, doorway transitions, or phone calls as authenticity cues.
- **Emotional signals:** Learning to use specific feelings as triggers for authentic reconnection rather than reactivity.
- **Body awareness:** Recognizing physical tension or other sensations as reminders to check authentic alignment.

These environmental triggers distribute your authentic living practice throughout your day, creating multiple brief opportunities for realignment rather than relying solely on dedicated practice sessions. They weave authenticity into the fabric of daily experience rather than segregating it as a separate activity.

Technology Supports: Digital Tools for Awareness

While technology often undermines authentic presence, strategic use of digital tools can actually support sustainable practice:

- **Mindfulness apps:** Programs designed specifically to support authentic presence and awareness.
- **Custom reminders:** Personalized notifications aligned with your specific authentic living intentions.
- **Tracking supports:** Simple ways to notice patterns in your authentic alignment over time.
- **Community platforms:** Digital connections with others pursuing similar authentic living paths.
- **Learning resources:** Online programs, videos, or courses that refresh and deepen your authentic living understanding.

These technology supports can serve as bridges between more direct authentic living practices, providing structure and reminders that maintain continuity in your alignment journey. The key is using technology intentionally as a support rather than allowing it to become a distraction from direct experience.

Environment Design: Authenticity Cues

Your physical and digital environments can be intentionally designed to cue and reinforce authentic living:

- **Value reminders:** Visual representations of core values placed in frequently seen locations.
- **Nature elements:** Plants, natural materials, or nature views that support present-moment awareness.
- **Sensory supports:** Elements that engage your senses in ways that promote centeredness.
- **Space organization:** Physical arrangements that facilitate rather than impede authentic activities.
- **Digital design:** Screen backgrounds, bookmarks, or other digital elements that reinforce authentic intentions.

These environmental designs reduce the cognitive load of remembering to practice authentic living, instead creating spaces that naturally evoke and support aligned presence. They transform your surroundings from potential distractions into active supports for your authentic expression.

Deepening Practices Over Time

Sustainable authentic living isn't static but evolves and deepens through continued engagement. Understanding how this development typically unfolds helps you recognize and support your progress rather than becoming discouraged by apparent plateaus or changes in your practice.

Baseline Shifting: Evolution of "Normal"

One of the most significant but subtle signs of progress is the gradual shift in your baseline state—what feels normal and natural to you:

- **Awareness normalization:** Emotional and physical sensations previously outside conscious recognition becoming regularly noticeable.
- **Expression evolution:** Authentic communication feeling increasingly natural rather than requiring deliberate effort.
- **Recovery acceleration:** Return to alignment after deviation happening more quickly and easily.
- **Discomfort with incongruence:** Growing natural discomfort with inauthentic patterns that previously felt normal.
- **Intuitive guidance:** Authentic choices arising spontaneously rather than requiring analytical deliberation.

As you consistently engage in these authentic practices, a quiet revolution unfolds within you: your "normal" subtly changes. Sensations you once ignored become clear signals, honest expression flows without conscious effort, and you bounce back from misalignment with surprising ease. The dissonance of inauthenticity, once a familiar hum, now feels jarring, and your intuition guides you towards choices that resonate with your true self. This isn't just about understanding authenticity; it's about embodying it, weaving it into the fabric of your being. You're not just doing authenticity; you're becoming it, with each passing day, each conscious choice, each gentle return to your center, you redefine your baseline, creating a life where genuine living is not a chore, but your natural, empowered state.

> "Evolution is an editing process, not an authoring process." - Daniel Dennett.

Challenge Incorporation: Expanding Your Range

As foundational authentic living practices become established, you can gradually expand to include more challenging aspects:

- **Emotional expansion:** Working with increasingly difficult emotions as your capacity develops.
- **Relationship extension:** Bringing authentic expression into more challenging relational contexts.
- **Situational spread:** Maintaining alignment in a wider range of circumstances and environments.

- **Identity evolution:** Incorporating aspects of authentic self previously excluded from your identity.
- **Depth exploration:** Moving from surface-level authenticity to deeper layers of congruence.

This progressive incorporation prevents overwhelming yourself with challenges beyond your current capacity while ensuring continued growth rather than stagnation. It represents an expanding circle of authentic living that gradually encompasses more of your experience.

SUBTLETY DEVELOPMENT: FROM OBVIOUS TO NUANCED

Over time, authentic living practice typically evolves from addressing obvious incongruence to recognizing increasingly subtle forms of misalignment:

- **Micro-expressions:** Noticing fleeting moments of inauthenticity previously too brief to register.
- **Partial incongruence:** Recognizing mixed states where authenticity and inauthenticity coexist.
- **Subtle body awareness:** Detecting increasingly refined physical signals of alignment and misalignment.
- **Word-feeling congruence:** Noticing the subtle gap between words and their emotional undertones.
- **Value alignment precision:** Discerning finer distinctions in how choices align with core values.

This subtlety development represents the refinement of your awareness and expression rather than a fundamental change in approach. It's similar to how a musician moves from playing notes correctly to exploring nuances of timing, tone, and interpretation as technical facility develops.

INTEGRATION PROGRESSION: FROM DOING TO BEING

Perhaps the most significant deepening involves the shift from authentic living as deliberate practice to integrated way of being:

- **Conscious competence to unconscious competence:** Authentic responses becoming increasingly automatic.
- **Effort reduction:** Alignment requiring less deliberate energy as neural pathways strengthen.
- **Identity incorporation:** Authentic living becoming part of your self-concept rather than something you aspire to.
- **Spontaneous expression:** Authentic responses arising naturally without conscious deliberation.
- **Unified experience:** Decreasing sense of separation between "practice time" and "regular life".

This integration progression doesn't mean perfect authenticity becomes effortless, but rather that the fundamental orientation toward authentic living becomes your default setting rather than requiring constant deliberate choice. The practice becomes who you are rather than just what you do.

Advanced Approaches: Building on Foundations

As basic authentic living practices become well-established, more nuanced approaches become accessible:

- **Paradox navigation:** Working with seemingly contradictory aspects of authentic experience.
- **Systems awareness:** Recognizing how your authentic expression affects and is affected by broader systems.
- **Creative integration:** Finding unique expressions of authenticity suited to your particular gifts and circumstances.
- **Transpersonal dimensions:** Exploring how authentic living relates to spiritual or existential questions.
- **Leadership extension:** Actively fostering conditions for others' authentic expression.

These advanced approaches aren't necessary for meaningful authentic living but offer avenues for continued growth when foundational practices are well-established. They represent the natural evolution of authentic living from personal practice to broader perspective and contribution.

Creating Sustainable Motivation

Even with well-designed practices, sustainable authentic living requires ongoing motivation—not the brief enthusiasm of new beginnings but the deeper commitment that sustains practice through inevitable challenges and periods of seeming plateau.

Values Connection: Your Why Matters

Connecting authentic living practices to your core values creates motivation that endures beyond temporary feelings:

- **Purpose clarification:** Regularly revisiting why authentic living matters to you personally.
- **Value manifestation:** Noticing how authenticity allows expression of your deepest values.
- **Cost awareness:** Maintaining realistic recognition of what misalignment costs you.
- **Benefit attention:** Consciously noticing positive effects of authentic living.
- **Legacy consideration:** Reflecting on the longer-term impact of authentic living on your life story.

This values connection transforms authentic living from something you should do to something you want to do because it directly expresses and serves what matters most to you. It creates motivation based on alignment rather than obligation, dramatically increasing sustainability.

PROGRESS TRACKING: NOTICING YOUR JOURNEY

Sustainable motivation requires recognizing movement on your authentic living path, especially during periods when progress feels slow or uncertain:

- **Regular reflection:** Scheduled times to notice changes in your authentic expression.
- **Baseline comparisons:** Occasionally looking back to earlier points in your journey rather than just yesterday.
- **Success journaling:** Recording specific instances of authentic living, particularly in challenging circumstances.
- **Feedback integration:** Thoughtfully considering others' observations about changes they notice.
- **Milestone acknowledgment:** Marking significant shifts in your authentic living development.

This progress tracking prevents the discouragement that comes when growth happens too gradually to notice without deliberate attention. It creates evidence of your authentic living development that sustains motivation through inevitable difficult periods.

COMMUNITY SUPPORT: THE POWER OF SHARED JOURNEY

Few things support sustainable authentic living more powerfully than connection with others on similar paths:

- **Practice partners:** Specific relationships focused on mutual support for authentic living.
- **Learning communities:** Groups that study and explore authentic living principles together.
- **Accountability connections:** Relationships that include gentle, supportive check-ins about intentions.
- **Inspiration exchanges:** Sharing experiences, challenges, and breakthroughs with fellow travelers.
- **Identity reinforcement:** Being part of communities where authentic living is normalized and valued.

This community dimension provides encouragement, perspective, and belonging that significantly enhance sustainability. It transforms authentic living from a solo endeavor to a shared journey, with the motivation that naturally emerges from meaningful connection around common values.

INSPIRATION RENEWAL: FEEDING YOUR PRACTICE

Regular exposure to sources that refresh and deepen your understanding of authentic living helps maintain enthusiasm and perspective:

- **Wisdom traditions:** Teachings from various contemplative and philosophical approaches that illuminate authentic living.
- **Contemporary voices:** Books, podcasts, talks, or other resources from current authentic living teachers.
- **Artistic inspiration:** Creative works that express or evoke authentic presence and expression.
- **Natural connection:** Time in natural settings that inherently support authentic awareness.
- **Success stories:** Examples of authentic living in practice from others' experiences.

This inspiration renewal prevents your authentic living understanding from becoming stale or firm. It regularly infuses fresh perspective and energy into your practice, maintaining the combination of stability and growth that supports long-term engagement.

Meaningful Celebration: Acknowledging the Journey

How you mark progress significantly impacts sustainable motivation. Effective celebration involves:

- **Value-aligned recognition:** Acknowledging milestones in ways that reinforce rather than undermine authentic values.
- **Process appreciation:** Celebrating the journey and effort, not just outcomes.
- **Community sharing:** Including others in marking significant developments.
- **Gratitude practice:** Explicitly appreciating the conditions and support that enable your authentic living.
- **Forward integration:** Using celebration to reinforce continued practice rather than as an endpoint.

This meaningful celebration creates positive reinforcement cycles that support continued engagement with authentic living practices. It acknowledges that progress deserves recognition while ensuring that celebration itself reflects and reinforces your authentic values.

The Ongoing Adventure of Authentic Living

As we conclude this book to emotional alignment and authentic living, remember that this journey has no final destination—no point of perfect, permanent authenticity you'll eventually reach. Rather, it's an ongoing adventure of increasingly aligned living, with continuous discovery, adjustment, and deepening.

This never-ending nature isn't a discouragement but an invitation—an opportunity to approach authentic living not as a problem to solve once and for all but as a rich, evolving exploration of what it means to be fully human. Each moment of alignment, each return from misalignment, each new discovery about your authentic expression becomes not just a step toward some future state but a complete experience of authentic living available right now.

The practices, approaches, and perspectives we've explored throughout this guide aren't formulas for perfection but invitations to engagement—ways of showing up more fully, honestly, and effectively in your one precious life. As you continue integrating these approaches in your unique way, may you discover not just greater emotional alignment but the profound aliveness that emerges when you bring your whole self to your experience.

Living authentically in our complex world, with its relentless demands and myriad distractions, isn't about retreating to an isolated haven; it's about cultivating an inner sanctuary of clarity and integrity within the chaos. It's about navigating the intricate web of relationships, responsibilities, and societal pressures with a grounded sense of self. It's the daily practice of choosing integrity over expediency, connection over conformity, and truth over comfort, even when it feels challenging. This ongoing commitment to alignment transforms the complex world from a source of overwhelm into a canvas for authentic expression, allowing you to create meaningful connections, contribute your unique gifts, and experience a profound sense of purpose, not in spite of the world's complexities, but within them.

Ultimately, the journey of continuous self-discovery is a lifelong commitment to authenticity and emotional growth. By embracing this journey, you can cultivate a deeper connection with yourself and with others, leading to a more fulfilling and enriched life. As you navigate the complexities of modern relationships and societal expectations, the skills acquired through this journey—such as authentic communication and emotional regulation—will empower you to express your true self boldly and confidently.

Remember that authentic living is both deeply personal and inherently relational—a way of being that benefits not only your individual wellbeing but reverberates through your connections, communities, and the broader world. Each step you take toward greater alignment contributes, however subtly, to a culture where authentic expression becomes more possible for everyone.

Thank you for joining me on this exploration of emotional alignment and authentic living. I hope the practices and perspectives we've shared serve as valuable companions on your continuing journey toward a life of integrity, connection, and genuine presence.

www.ingramcontent.com/pod-product-compliance
Lightning Source LLC
Chambersburg PA
CBHW081252040426
42453CB00014B/2390